RUDOW'S GUIDE TO

ROCKFISH

BY LENNY RUDOW

D1125245

GEARED UP PUBLICATIONS, LLC
EDGEWATER, MD
WWW.GEAREDUPPUBLICATIONS.COM

This one's dedicated to Kari Snyder, whose tireless work and undefeatable attitude has helped make Geared Up a reality.

TABLE OF CONTENTS

INTRODUCTION

You want a dissertation on the historical importance of striped bass? Then go to the library, and look up "boring." You want to know the mating habits of Morone Saxatilis? Cool. Me, too. But that's not going to be a topic of discussion in Rudow's Guide to Rockfish. In fact, you will never again see the Latin name for this fish printed in this book—I couldn't care less what weird, irrelevant name some seventeenth-century biologist used to describe the fish that we call striper. Reality Check: the historical and scientific facts you'll find in here are only those that have a direct impact on how and when to maximize your angling productivity. This book is dedicated to one thing—helping you catch more striped bass. Make that two things, because I'm sure you want to catch bigger ones, too. In Rudow's Guide to Rockfish, we'll pick apart the factors that have an effect on the way you fish: tidal patterns, water quality, sun and moon, weather changes, and the like. We'll detail each of the major tactics used by recreational and professional anglers and discuss which is most effective when, where, and why. You'll learn my top 10 hotspots for catching stripers, and why each of these locations offers you an opportunity to enjoy the striper fishing of a lifetime. And yes, finally, we will get into proper catch and release methods. Because if we anglers don't do everything within our power to keep the striper stocks healthy, than our own sport is doomed.

The striped bass—rockfish, to anglers living in this fish's southern range—is the most popular inshore gamefish in the Mid Atlantic region. It's also one of the few success stories in interstate fisheries management. In 1982 the entire Atlantic striped bass population was estimated to total about five million, but after employing interstate management techniques including a complete ban on harvesting the fish, this number grew quickly. By 1995, the population broke 40 million. It continued to grow through '97, then more or less hit a plateau.

Back when striped bass were few and far between, the popularity of bluefish surpassed that of stripers among recreational anglers. Did people really like blues more than they did rock? Not likely, but it's hard for fishermen to fall in love with fish they can't find or catch. Luckily, these days we have plenty of stripers to chase after and anglers up and down the coast can reasonably hope for fish in the cooler on a regular basis. Speaking of fish in the cooler: few can hold a candle to rockfish when it's time to fire up the grill.

Okay, enough BS—let's get right down to brass tacks. It's time to catch more, bigger fish.

CHAPTER ONE

STRIPER SCIENCE
What you need to know about this species to target it more effectively.

Unlike many species of fish found in the Atlantic Ocean and nearby bays, we actually know a fair amount about striped bass. We know when and where they spawn, their major migration routes, feeding habits, and basic behavioral patterns. And we anglers can—and should—use this knowledge to our advantage.

A striper on the feed—come and get it!

It's incredibly important to remember that the knowledge you'll gain about biological factors that influence the striped bass's behavior, alone, will not fill your fishbox. Nor will your understanding of the influence of tides and currents, water temperature, light levels, and any of the other specific fish-affecting factors we're going to get into here, if you consider them in a vacuum. All of these elements are in play at all times. Some will be more prominent than others in particular situations, and will be less important at other times. You have to consider all of these influences at once, and try to understand the entire web of factors impacting the fish's behavior at any given moment. Putting all of the pieces of the puzzle together to gain a fuller understanding of what the fish are doing and why they are doing it is paramount to success.

A brief review of the basics: The striped bass is commonly called rockfish, or striper. They average one to five pounds, but 10 and 15 pound fish are relatively common. Much larger fish—up to 60-pounds and above—will be encountered on occasion. The world record hook-and-line caught striper was a hair over 78 pounds, but catches nearing 100 pounds have been claimed by commercial fishermen. By noting their seasonal migration routes and the timing of the spawn, anglers can target the largest fish of the species. Is that a good thing? For the guy with the bent rod, at that moment, yes. But we have to be careful. As we've seen many times before, removing the big cow fish from the spawning stock has a dramatic impact on the long term prospects of the fishery. Note, for example, that a sexually mature female striped bass weighing about 10 pounds can spawn over a half-million eggs each spring. That's a nice fish, and this is a lot of eggs, right? Sure. But a 50 pound cow will lay some four million eggs. You could harvest eight of the 10-pounders, or 80 total pounds of striped bass, before having the same impact on the spawning stock as harvesting that single 50 pound fish. On top of that, if you're harvesting 10 pound fish many of them will be males, which top out around 30 pounds. But if you're taking 50 pounders, all are bound to be females. So in the long run, it's clearly better for the fishery to leave the biggest of the big fish alone.

Don't get me wrong; I wouldn't deny anyone the opportunity to take home their "fish of a lifetime," and if I caught a new world record rock you can bet I'd take it to the scales... before eating it. But we'll all be a lot happier in the long run if we regularly release the 40, 50, and 60 pound fish, and make killing that fish of a lifetime just that—a once in a lifetime event. Bearing this information in mind, and if you want to land a real trophy, keeping tabs on the migration patterns and spawning patterns of the big cows will enable you to target them at the appropriate time in the appropriate place.

Migration Patterns

By most estimates, slightly more than half of all the stripers along the Atlantic seaboard are born in the Chesapeake Bay and its tributaries. Like many anadromous fish, (those which spawn in freshwater but live out their lives in salt or brackish water) stripers return to the river or creek where they were born, to propagate the next generation. Scientists will argue back and forth about the exact num-

---

Bonus Factoid

Well before the Maryland trophy striper season starts (usually in mid April,) these big stripers can be effectively targeted on a catch-and-release basis. In fact, some people suspect that during mild years some of these fish over-winter in the bay itself. Virtually every year you'll be able to catch them as early as February or March. Look to find these cold-weather fish at warm-water discharges when the bay water temperatures are hovering in the upper 30's to the lower 40's. When the temps are in the mid and upper 40's you'll be able to find these big fish throughout the bay, under small flocks of diving gannets.

ber which return to the bay each spring, but estimates range from 50 percent to 80 percent of the entire Atlantic stock. The Susquehanna is the king of all striper spawning rivers, and other Chesapeake tributaries with strong spawning runs include the Chester, Choptank, James, Nanticoke, Potomac, Rappahannock, and York Rivers. After spawning, most of the large stripers migrate back to the ocean and travel up the coast to feed in the bait-rich northern waters of New Jersey, New York, and Massachusetts. Smaller "resident" fish remain in the Chesapeake through the seasons, but many start migrating in just a few years and the majority of the fish join the migration by the time they reach 30" in length. Several rivers in North Carolina—most notably the Roanoke and the Cape Fear—also have strong striper runs. To the north, the biggest run occurs in New York's Hudson River, with smaller runs taking place in the Delaware River and New Jersey's coastal tributaries.

Knowing this, it shouldn't surprise you that during the early spring the Chesapeake holds top honors for finding cow stripers. The vast majority are taken by trolling, but chumming with well-honed techniques which were developed by my family and I during the late 90's can be successfully employed as well (more on this later, in chapter 7).

Once the big breeders have migrated out of the bay, usually during the month of May when water temperatures reach the mid and upper 60's, Chesapeake anglers will be left with mostly resident fish. Some seasons there are strong late-spring, summer, or fall runs of fish in the 30" to 36" class in the bay, but catching any fish over this size range once July hits is a rarity. So the prime time to take a trophy here is from the season opening through part or all of May.

Meanwhile, anglers on the hunt for big fish should also be paying attention to the Delaware, New Jersey, and New York coasts. Beginning in mid to late April most seasons, the first of the big fish that have already left the Chesapeake can be intercepted as they migrate up the coast. At the same time, big post-spawn stripers coming from the Hudson, the Delaware Bay, and other smaller tributaries and rivers with spawning stocks also work their way up the coast.

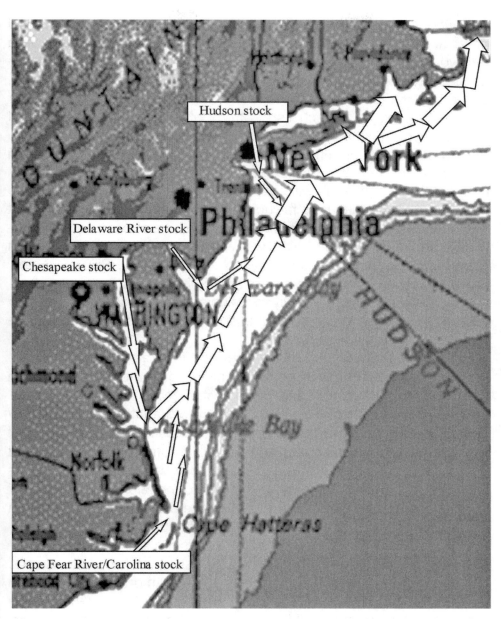

As the spring migration takes place, fish from several stocks move north and intermingle.

The Chesapeake's early season will overshadow the runs in these other areas, but after the bay's trophy season has been underway for two or three weeks, the bite in northern points will start picking up steam; sooner or later it will surpass that on the bay. As the bulk of the big fish leave the Chesapeake and move up the coast all of the stocks mix, and which fish is from which breeding ground becomes anyone's guess. The surf and near-shore bite picks up along the coast, and by the time May hits there will be a good number of big fish appearing around Montauk, New York. Within a few weeks, many of these same fish will keep working their way north and eventually, some will make it as far up the coast as the Bay of Fundy.

During this time frame the waters of Massachusetts and Rhode Island, particularly around Martha's Vineyard, Nantucket Sound, and Cape Cod, become the best places to find trophy stripers. Here, these fish will be caught by trollers and by live-baiting with large herring or bunker. The bite usually remains strong until warmer weather sets in, and large numbers of bluefish make it harder and harder to target the stripers specifically.

These fish will feed all summer and into the fall, before working their way south again. The large fish will become more scattered once summer hits, and coastal areas with lighted bridges become a favorite of night fishermen willing to stay awake late to get in on the best action. From the farthest northern reaches of the range, stripers will head back down the coast in mid to late September. At some point in October the feeding will peak in New York waters, with the best of the big fish hunts usually taking place around the northern end of Long Island. As the water cools and the bite drops off, fishing in New Jersey coastal waters becomes better and better. The hot bite along the beach usually lasts for a month or so, as the bulk of the stock will move south. Eventually the schools of fish will slow their travels, and spend the winter somewhere from the mouth of the Chesapeake down to North Carolina. If Maryland anglers are lucky some of the ocean-run fish will move all the way up into the middle-Chesapeake before the end of this state's season. More reliably, winter fishing for trophy-sized fish takes place in Virginia's portion of the bay and coast and North Carolina's coastal waters, and at times will be every bit as productive as any other trophy fishery in the Atlantic region. You want to catch a big bass on New Years day? Many seasons you can pull it off, if you head for Virginia Beach or the Outer Banks.

If you want to learn more about striper migrations, one place you should visit is www.stripertracker.org. This web site gives you the ability to tap into a fascinating study performed by scientists at Rutgers University, tracking the migration patterns of stripers from New Jersey's Mullica River and coastal bays.

There are a few oddball striper stocks which should also be mentioned because to some anglers, these are fish of great importance. The first is the west coast stock, which mostly spawns in the San Joaquin and Sacramento Rivers. The fish here spawn slightly later than their east coast counterparts, usually from April through June.

Striped bass have also been introduced into many inland reservoirs but for the most part, have not established self-sustaining populations. Two notable exceptions are Kerr Reservoir in Virginia and Santee-Cooper in South Carolina. In both of these freshwater lakes, healthy populations of stripers reproduce every year.

Stripes & Teeth

Take one look at a striper, and from then on you'll never have trouble identifying these fish. Those zebra-like lines across their flanks, bass-like jaws, and chunky body make it nearly impossible to confuse a rock with any other fish in the Atlantic. But, why do these fish have stripes? And more importantly, why should you care? Remember—understanding the fish will help you find and catch it.

The stripes on a striper's sides visually break up the shape of the fish. Even though they look uniform to us and it may seem that the stripes advertise their presence instead of camouflaging it, underwater they have the effect of interrupting the fish's body characteristics. This is especially true when refracted light shimmers on the bottom or structure the fish is hiding or feeding near. In fact, these

The striper's sandpaper-like teeth makes handling them by the jaw easy—and should tip you off as to what and how they eat.

factors partially explain why some people call striped bass rockfish, and why the fish carries its scientific name (you know what it is—we don't have to start talking in Latin again,) which means "rock dwell-er."

Stripers are often found at or around rocks of all types, and one of the reasons why is the ability of the fish to blend into the shadows and uneven rock surfaces. When viewed from above, the striper's greenish back and striped sides disappear. When viewed from below the white underbelly blends with the light coming from the surface. What's it all mean to us? It may be a bit obvious, but take the lesson to heart—stripers are structure-oriented fish, and more often than not you'll find them clinging tight to sub-surface structure. Of course, there are exceptions. Fish swimming up the surf, or high in the water column to migrate, for example. But generally speaking you'll find these fish feeding hardest and spending much their time around rocks and other solid structure. Bridge pilings, rip-rap, under-water rocks and rock piles, and jetties are a few examples of rocky rockfish hotspots.

The teeth of a striped bass provide another clue as to how to catch these fish. Stripers have sandpaper-like teeth, which makes handling them by the jaw relatively easy. Stripers have these teeth as opposed to sharp, cutting teeth, because they feed not by biting and slicing their pray but by sucking it in and grabbing it; most meals are swallowed whole. Some favorites of the striped bass include: eels, soft or peeler crabs, menhaden, spot, bloodworms, clams, and her-ring.

Whether you're using bait or lures, always bear the striper's teeth and the corresponding feeding tactics in mind. Picture that fish sucking in its meal, then clamping tightly for several seconds to in-jure or kill the bait. Only then will the striper gulp it down. Now ask yourself: are you planning to harvest the fish you catch? If you're fishing with bait and you let the fish eat for several seconds after you feel the initial strike, you'll be a lot more likely to get a solid hook-up. Remember—first the rockfish sucks and grabs, then it clamps down, then it swallows. On the flip side, letting the fish eat also means you're more likely to gut-hook it. The bottom line? When you plan to release the fish or when you're catching throw-backs mixed in with the keepers, set the hook more quickly to prevent hurting the fish that will be thrown back.

Just how long should you give a fish to eat a bait? Official disclaimer: this will change in different conditions, according to how they influence the fish's behavior. In 80 degree water, for example, a striper will eat a lot faster than it will in 50 degree water. So consider the following list a broad generalization.

• Bloodworm, clam snouts, crab chunks, clam, and other relatively small baits: set the hook upon feeling a solid strike. In cold water when fishing whole bloodworms for large stripers, allow the fish a second or two to suck it all the way in.

• Medium or small menhaden chunks in a chum line: set the hook immediately. Note—allowing the fish to eat chunks in a chum line regularly leads to gut-hooked fish.

• Peanut bunker, small spot, and other live baits under four inches: three to five seconds for fish in the 18" to 26" class, and two to three seconds for larger fish.

• Live eels: five seconds, or until the bumping sensation of the grab-and-hold period turns into the steady pull of the fish swimming away, after it's swallowed the bait.

• Large menhaden chunks such as heads or fist-sized fillets: five seconds.

• Large live baits such as bunker, spot, croaker, or herring over six inches: five to seven seconds.

Lures, naturally, don't require any wait-time beyond the initial strike. In fact, with most lures waiting to set the hook will only give the fish a chance to realize something isn't right, and spit the hook.

What more can we learn from those sandpaper-like teeth? Wire leaders or heavy mono intended to prevent cut-offs is unnecessary. Rockfish can't bite through fishing line, and will take a very long time to weaken it through abrasion. Since wire or thick mono is more visible than light mono leaders and will cut down on the number of strikes you get, eliminate it from the mix when you're targeting stripers. This factor is less important when trolling since the fish have less time to eyeball a leader when the lure passes by.

This fact leads us to another biological trait of the striped bass which anglers should pay close attention to: the size of their eyes. Stripers have relatively good vision, and will see thick or wire leaders better than some other species. They are also adept at feeding in low-light conditions. Striped bass usually feed better at night than they do during the day. So, why do we catch so many during the day? Because that's when the bulk of the anglers are on the water. If you spend a few nights striper fishing, you'll quickly discover that they do in fact get quite active at night. In certain conditions, when light levels, temperatures, water quality conditions and bait behavior all conspire to make daytime feeding difficult for the rockfish, they may feed almost exclusively during the dark. Blue-bird skies and bright sunlight can be down-right uncomfortable for these fish at times, and may hinder feeding or force the fish to move lower in the water column. In fact, light levels are so important to assessing the striped bass's behavior that we'll dedicate a lot more space to this factor shortly. For now, just remember those big eyes, and how important they are to understanding why stripers behave the way they do.

One other factor you should be aware of: Large stripers are relatively lazy fish. They will and do scavenge whenever possible, and prefer to gulp down injured or dead meals as opposed to chasing after fish. So, if this is the case, why do they chase lures? For one thing, there's not a lure in the world that actually looks 100-percent like a healthy fish swimming through the water. That wobbling spoon, paddling tail, or twisting twister may look life-like, but it doesn't look "normal." Often when the striper sees your lure it thinks it's damaged or injured pray, which (hopefully) triggers the fish to attack. In fishing parlance, this is usually called a "reaction strike," and explains why there are times when some lures will out-fish some natural baits.

Another thing you should remember about the lazy factor is that when smaller fish and larger fish are in the same area, you'll generally catch the larger fish deeper and the smaller fish shallower. Those little guys are full of energy and spunk, and they're willing to chase bait right up the surface. Bigger fish, meanwhile, will calmly cruise below and wait for injured or dead baitfish which escaped or sunk un-noticed from the surface frenzy, to provide them with a free meal.

The final reason you should keep their slothful tendencies in mind is because there are times and places when dead cut bait will actually out-fish live baits of the exact same type and size. It sounds weird but it's true, particularly when the fish are in migration mode or have run up-stream into relatively freshwater bodies of water.

Every time you fish keep all of the rockfish's habits in mind. Each provides you with one more piece to the puzzle—and you need each and every piece to fit together if your cooler's going to be full by the end of the trip.

CHAPTER TWO

SUNLIGHT, MOON PHASE, AND TIDAL INFLUENCES
Don't fish in a vacuum.

You want to catch more fish than the competition? The single most important thing you can do is go fishing earlier and/or stay out later in the day. Time your arrival at the initial spot you plan on fishing with the first crack of light on the horizon. If you wait until it's light out to run your boat, you've just missed out on prime fishing time. Same goes for sunset. Often you'll see boat after boat pull in its lines and run for home as the sun nears the horizon. Little do these anglers know, they're about to miss one of the best fishing times of the entire day. The old-timers call it "two fingers from the horizon." Hold your hand out at arms' length with two fingers extended. When the sun is less than two fingers over the horizon, the fish are about to go into feeding mode.

If you're fishing shallows or flats, timing your fishing to occur with low-light periods is even more important. Ambient light means a hot bite—and when the sun is high in the sky, that bite drops off to a shadow of what it was during the first hour of fishing. There will, of course, be exceptions. A completely dead tide at sunrise and a rip-roaring tide at noon, for example, can turn this rule upside-down and on its head. But generally speaking, with all other things being equal, stripers bite five or even 10 times better in ambient light then in direct light. You absolutely, positively can't get out on the water early? If you hope to catch fish in the shallows, look for shaded water. Docks, trees close to shore, bulkheads, and moored boats all provide shade that fish prowling the shoreline will orient to. If you're not fishing the shallows, then you're more likely to find the fish high in the water column during the low-light hours, and low in the water column during the bright light periods. That's why you'll find fish breaking water more often on cloudy days than on sunny days. It's also why you'll see more and more schools of fish pop up on the surface as the sun drops on the horizon and light levels go down. Of course there are exceptions—if a school of fish works a patch of bait to the surface and can effectively feed on it, they certainly will do so even if the sun is beaming down. But as a general rule of thumb, remember to look high in the water during low light, and low in the water during bright light.

Lucky for you and I, the low-light conditions created by cloud cover can be nearly as good for striper fishing as the low-light conditions created by daybreak and sunset. Some days, it'll extend that hot bite right through the entire solar cycle. As you plan where and when to fish, however, remember that there can be a reverse-effect from lighting conditions, as well. Let's say, for example, the day brought heavy cloud cover and a health striper bite. Night fishing that evening may not be your best bet, since the fish have full bellies. And on the day following a clear, calm, full-moon night, catching rockfish can sometimes seem impossible. Again, it's because the fish had perfect feeding conditions prior to when you went on the hunt, so they aren't very interested in eating. Should conditions like these stop you from fishing? Heck no! But what if you have your choice between fishing on day A or day B? Day A is preceded by a calm, clear, bright night, and day B is preceded by a dark cloudy night. Choosing which day to fish just got a little easier—and you'll catch more fish for making the correct decision.

The effect of light must play a role in your on-the-spot decisions, as well. If clouds or a low-light morning give way to direct sunlight as you troll, and the lures that were getting smashed near the surface suddenly go untouched, add weight or change your offerings to get them deeper in the water column. If you're chumming and the bites that were strong on un-weighted baits fished near the surface suddenly drop off, consider adding some lead to those lines. You had success jigging along the top of a drop-off, but when the sun came out the fish quit? Look to find them deeper along that same drop, before moving on or changing tactics. Sometimes, a change of just three or four feet of depth is all it takes to get your offering back into the strike zone. Other times, you'll find the fish have adjusted by a larger margin. It takes some experimentation to figure out exactly where the fish have moved to, but by remembering the effect of direct sunlight you'll find the fish a lot faster than you would simply by guessing.

Moon Phase

The phase of the moon also has a huge impact on the fish, and how they will behave. Naturally, much of this influence is tied into the moon's effect on tides and currents. But not all of it.

The first effect one must consider is the amount of illumination provided by the moon. This will have a big impact on the effectiveness of night fishing. As mentioned earlier, stripers often bite better at night than they do during the day. This is particularly true during the warmest months of the year. During the dog days of July and August, night fishing is often ten times better than fishing during the day.

There are two distinct and conflicting schools of thought on this matter. The first is that the bigger the moon is and the more illumination it provides, the better the fishing will be. The second is that the smaller the moon is and the less illumination it provides, the more effect artificial lights will have in drawing fish in to concentrated areas, making them easier to catch. There's a kernel of truth to both theories. In the light of a full moon, night lights definitely do not draw in fish quite as effectively as they do during a half or quarter or obscured moon. Bridge light-lines (one of the best places to night fish for stripers) do not concentrate the fish as dramatically, and the stripers seem to have an easier time of finding meals on their own. Yet the increased tidal action that comes with the full moon does stimulate more active feeding patterns, and you can catch a heck of a lot of fish during the full moon.

On the flip side of the coin, when there's very little moonlight stripers will congregate in huge numbers around light-lines, lighted piers, and night lights set out by anglers. Are you asking yourself "which is the better time to fish?" If so, you're asking the wrong question. The question that will lead to a fuller fishbox is "which is the most effective way to target the fish in the conditions I'm presented with?" If the moon's bright and the currents are strong, work an area that you'd expect to find fish feeding in during broad daylight—a rip, rockpile, or shelf. But when the moon is dim and the current is wimpy, look for an area that draws in the fish and puts them into a feeding mood, such a bridge light-lines or artificially lighted piers. Note that anglers who carry their own night fishing lights (we'll cover this topic in greater detail in chapter 10) can turn the daytime/full moon hotspot into a productive area with their lights, during periods of dim moonlight. Also note, however, that the fish know where the usual light areas are and will head for them first in these conditions; it may take a couple of hours for the full effects of artificial lights to kick in, if you're in an area where there isn't usually artificial lighting. The best-case scenario? Intermittent cloud-cover, interrupting the light of a full moon. This situation will provide you with strong tides and good current, plus an enhanced fish-attracting ability for your artificial lights.

Direct lighting is not the only effect of the lunar cycle which you must take into account. Again, it must be stressed: all of these factors come together to create a web of influences, and you need to consider the effect of them all taken as a whole. Another factor the moon triggers which will have a huge impact on the striped bass's behavior is the lunar effect on other creatures. May worms, for example, have a life cycle which is ruled by the moon. And when the May worms hatch, fishing will change radically.

May worms, correctly called polychaetes, are the small red worms sometimes called clam worms, or mud worms. They are very similar to the bloodworms we use for bait, and there are many different species found throughout the Mid Atlantic region. Most are commonly two or three inches long, but can grow as large as five or six inches in length. During the month of May they engage in their first spawn of the year. (But not the only one; several other hatches will follow as the season progresses). The May worms metamorphose into "heteronereises," the sex stage of their life. They grow enlarged fins that allow them to swim off of the bottom, and up towards the surface. Here, they swarm in huge schools to mate. Since they're attracted to light one can watch this process, if you have access to a lighted pier or put lights out on your own boat during this cycle. It only lasts for a few days, then the spawned worms die—or get eaten by striped bass. In fact, the reason the May worm hatch is important to you is that stripers will go into an intense feeding mode during it, and gorge themselves silly. It may become nearly impossible to catch a fish, because they have such an easy time eating the May worms they simply aren't interested in eating anything else. Fish you are able to pull into the boat will often regurgitate bellies full of May worms. Fortunately for us, this scenario usually plays itself out after a day or two of uninhibited eating. Note that during this phase, when it gets really tough to catch stripers on the usual lures or baits, a small piece of red yarn is often more effective as bait than that chunk of menhaden or soft crab.

Wait a sec—did we say soft crab? What a great segue to the next lunar effect you need to bear in mind: the blue crab molt. There is some debate as to exactly when and why the first blue crab molt of the year occurs, but there's no question that stripers love eating soft crab and once the molt kicks in, fishing will be effected dramatically. Traditionally, commercial watermen and others with close ties to the water have used the "dogwood theory" to predict the occurrence of that first molt: when the dogwoods bloom, the crabs start shedding. This time frame usually coincides with two other factors that appear to have a clear bearing on blue crab molting, water temperature and the full moon of May. Crabs begin to shed when the water hits 59 degrees. Since shallow water warms more quickly than deep water, and since geography can play a significant role in water temperature, the effect is not limited to a tight time period in any specific place. In fact, crabs may begin molting early in May in some areas and in late May in others. Crabs in Virginia's portion of the Chesapeake, for example, usually molt about two weeks before those in the upper reaches of the bay. So the molt is clearly not triggered or defined by the full moon alone.

Scientists have two potential answers as to why. The first theory notes that blue crabs won't molt until their body is well-fed. The full moon of May brings higher than usual tides, allowing the crabs to move farther up into the marsh banks and feed heavily. Thus, as the tides increase the crabs get closer and closer to bursting. The second theory also focuses on the higher than usual tides, but considers the defenseless nature of crabs when they molt. They need to have grasses to hide in, and the access to additional hiding territory provided by the high tides triggers the process.

There's just one problem with all of the theories related to the reasons they molt at this time: scientists have found that crabs held in the lab molted significantly more around the period of a full moon, even through there's no change of lighting, food availability, or cover for them to hide in. Bottom line: no one can say for sure exactly what's going on, but there will be more crabs molting around the time of a full moon than there will be at other times of the month.

Why is all this molt stuff important to you? Remember, it will have a huge effect on stripers and the ways and places they feed. Try fishing soft or peeler crab prior to the first significant molt, and you'll discover that other baits fished side-by-side with it will usually catch more fish. Switch over to soft crab during the appropriate lunar cycle when the molt is in full swing, and the fish will slurp it down like candy. An example: on several occasions we've gone to great lengths (and paid big bucks!) to acquire fresh soft crab during the early period of the trophy striper season on the Chesapeake. Fishing with a half of a soft crab on two lines and cut menhaden on two lines, in all cases the menhaden out-fished the crab two or three to one. Eventually, we stopped working so hard to get soft crab into the mix at this time of the season. But in mid-May we religiously add soft crab into the mix and it generally does as well as the menhaden chunks. There is a period of a week or so—could it just be coincidence that it coincides with a full moon?—during which the crab catches more fish than the menhaden, hands-down.

Another reason to stay in tune with the molt is that it will help you better predict where the rockfish are going to be going on the hunt. During peak molting weeks, you can expect to find larger numbers of fish in the shallows. This even holds true for migrating fish. Although they don't seem to spend a whole lot of time specifically seeking out feeding areas, you will find that as the molt peaks big stripers turn up in very, very shallow water. Along rip-rapped shores and near those with heavy weed cover adjacent to open water (as opposed to up tributaries or in creeks) trophy-sized fish will pop up quite often. Naturally, since we're talking about the shallows it's most common for the fish to move in here right at dusk and right at sunrise. It's not unusual for early season croaker anglers, casting bloodworm chunks on bottom rigs, to accidentally intercept these fish—and every good croaker angler knows the evening bite, when the sun is low or below the horizon—is best.

Tidal Influences

Naturally, as most anglers will already know, the greatest impact the moon has on striper fishing comes from the tidal cycles. Since the moon travels in an elliptical pattern around the Earth, these cycles have periods during which they are stronger, and others during which they are weaker. Spring tides are the strongest, and occur when the moon and the sun are in line with each other, maximizing gravitational pull on the water. These tides create currents of maximum intensity with shorter durations. When the moon and sun are at right angles, neap tides occur. These are the weakest of the tides, and they create weaker currents which have longer periods of maximum intensity.

Just to avoid any confusion, at this point we should differentiate between tides and currents. They are not exactly the same thing, and these two terms are often used interchangeably even though they have different meanings. Tide is the vertical movement of water level, and is properly used to describe the height of the water. To say "at high tide the water is at its highest point," is accurate. To say "the tide is creating an eddy," however, is not accurate. The horizontal movement of water is called current, and when most of us talk about moving water and the effect it has on fishing, current is what we are referring to. In fact, while tide changes certainly have the majority of the influence on currents, they are not the lone cause. Wind-driven current occurs often and in some cases may even out-weigh the tidal influence. Anyone who spends a good deal of time around the shoreline has seen strong winds blow the water out of rivers, creeks, and bays. Currents can also be man-made. Draining locks, for example, creates current, and even propwash could accurately be considered current.

While this may seem like splitting hairs, it's worth talking about because this knowledge will help you catch more fish. Case in point: night fishing around marinas and docks. If you can locate a dock or marina which has regularly timed boat traffic—ferry docks, for example—you've discovered a man-made current which is strong enough and reliable enough to become noteworthy... to the fish, that is. Whenever the ferry pulls off the dock, its propwash will stir up the bottom, washing small worms, crabs, shrimp, and other tiny critters high into the water column. If this happens on a regular, frequent basis, the fish in the area absolutely, positively, will become conditioned to it. You can guess what happens next: the predators move in for an easy kill when that current kicks up. If you're on the spot ready and waiting with a baited hook the moment that ferry pulls off the dock, and you toss that bait into that manmade current that's washing up the food, you have a great shot at hooking up with a fish. This tactic works particularly well in areas with relatively low currents, or during dead periods of the tide when there's little current running elsewhere.

Of course, there is a limited number of places and times where man-made currents regularly apply. More commonly, the current-creation most anglers will be looking for is a naturally occurring rip. Rips are areas of standing or disturbed water which are easily recognized by the presence of waves or ripples in the area. They are caused when moving water slams into structure, bottom changes, opposing currents, or points of land. In the waters around Cape Cod or Martha's Vineyard, for example, rips are often created by shoals and sand bars adjacent to deeper water. In Long Island Sound, rips are likely to be formed by rock ledges, or reefs. And in the back-bays of the Jersey coast, the Chesapeake's shallows, and the Albemarle Sound, rips often form around points and outcroppings of island and marsh banks. All of these areas will (at the correct point in the season and taking the other applicable variables into account) hold rockfish.

To properly fish a current rip with lures, one must understand its anatomy. Any current-created surface rip, regardless of what form the structure creating it takes, can be broken down into several differ-

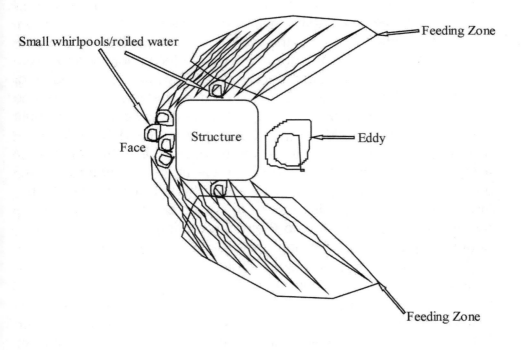

The anatomy of a current-generated surface rip, viewed from overhead: its face, structure, eddy, and feeding zones.

ent sections. The face of the rip is the section where the current actually meets the structure. Often, small whirlpools, waves, and other surface disturbances are visible. Although you may draw a strike or two by casting into the face of a rip, this is not the primary feeding zone. If you make a cast at the feeding zone and hit the face, however, much of the time the current will naturally take your offering into the feeding zone. You may be able to wait for a few seconds and allow the current to do its work, then begin your retrieve and effectively draw your offering through the feeding zone. The limiting factor here is the weight of your lure or bait. If your offering will sink and hit bottom or the structure before reaching the hotspot, there's a good chance the fish won't see it or it will become snagged.

The eddy of the rip is the pocket of calm, protected water behind the structure. Rips that form around points as opposed to structure often won't have visible eddies, but will have a calm pocket of water inside the rip. (The face, feeding zone, and the rip itself will be the same when forming off a point, except that it will occur on a single side instead of each side of the structure.) Fish will often hold in eddies and calm areas, but this is not the area where they feed most actively. Yes, I know, many people believe that this is where the fish are, and thus should be your target area. This is a commonly held but incorrect belief. In fact, fish that sit in eddies continually are inactive and those on the hunt spend their time darting from the eddy into, out of, and across the feeding zone. So why have you caught fish, while casting into eddies? Because casting into them will still lead to success if you retrieve your offering up-current or cross-current, out of the eddy and into the feeding zone. This is an accidental but real result which perpetuates the myth. When you understand how the fish holding around rips and eddies behave, however, you'll quickly discover that you can catch more fish by focusing on the feeding zone, in the first place. If you're observant, you may have noticed that when you are positioned down-current and cast up into a rip, you almost never catch fish. That's because your lure never passes through that magic feeding zone. Even worse, your lure is traveling with the current and most of the time, baitfish will be facing into the

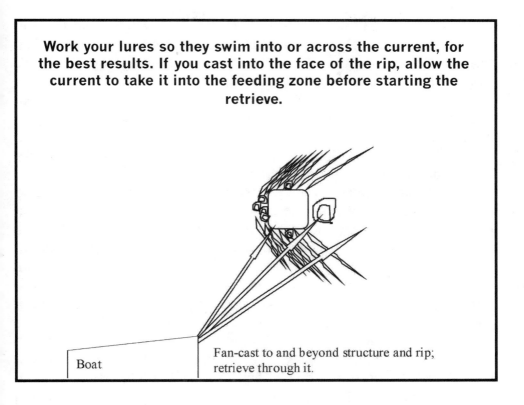

Work your lures so they swim into or across the current, for the best results. If you cast into the face of the rip, allow the current to take it into the feeding zone before starting the retrieve.

Boat

Fan-cast to and beyond structure and rip; retrieve through it.

current. Your lure looks unnatural, does not travel through the area where feeding fish are hunting, and the fishbox stays empty.

Why are the feeding zones of a rip off to the sides of the eddy and structure? Picture the rockfish holding in the eddy, watching the feeding zone. As tidbits of food and baitfish are flushed past, they dart out of the eddy and into the current to grab the hapless critters being swept around the structure. The stronger the current is, the less distance the fish will usually swim from the eddy to grab a bait. In a roaring four knot current, you may need to place that bucktail dead in the feeding zone and within a foot or two of the eddy to get a strike. When the current is weaker, fish will swim farther out of the eddy with less urgency and hesitation. Unfortunately, at this stage of the tide they're usually feeding less intensely, too.

Regardless of which section of the rip you're trying to cast to, position yourself so your lures are always being retrieved into or across the current. Remember, baitfish don't often swim directly with the current and stripers will act dubious about hitting anything that's swimming in the wrong direction.

The manner in which you approach a rip is important, too, because those fish can hear a lot more than most people think. Experiment for yourself by approaching in stealth mode and approaching loudly, and you'll discover the difference in your catch is drastic, particularly when you're fishing in shallow water.

The first mistake most people make is talking loudly, jumping on and off casting decks, and opening and closing coolers, rodboxes, or tackleboxes. During testing for a Boating Magazine article, we took hydrophone db-A level readings five to 10' below the surface, 30' behind the boat, and discovered that people talking in a loud but normal voice were completely audible. Underwater db-A level measurements also proved that a 24-volt, 72-pound thrust electric motor was quieter than a two-stroke outboard, especially if the motor is shifted into neutral. (Two-strokes made nearly double the volume in neutral, as opposed to in forward gear at idle.) If a two-stroke is your only power option then you're best off by idling into position, shutting the motor off without shifting out of forward gear, and dropping an anchor or starting your drift. Don't re-start the motor until you've fished-out the spot or have drifted away from it. In any case, don't just drift along with a two-stroke idling away. The same was not true when we measured sound levels with a four-stroke outboard. It made even less noise than the 24-volt electric, so long as it was run it at idle. Above about 1500 rpm (for gasoline-powered outboards) or 60-percent throttle (for an electric) prop noise started to outweigh all the other sounds the powerplants were creating, anyway. A 12-volt, 36-lb thrust motor is about as stealthy as it gets. Naturally, the down-side is that it doesn't have much power, and is ineffective for aluminum boats over 16' or so and fiberglass or poly boats over about 14'.

Allowing a hatch to slam shut is the worst offender of all, not only in volume but also in terms of spooking the fish. Try it for yourself the next time fish are visible from your boat—nothing sends them darting like the sharp sound of fiberglass smacking fiberglass.

One more item to consider when going into stealth mode: your depth finder. Most people, including many engineers who design and build depth finders, do not believe that fish can hear them. I disagree. During field work for an article, I once had the opportunity to launch a small boat into the massive tank in the National Aquarium in Baltimore. While a second person watched from two stories below, I switched on and off several different depth finders. All were relatively low-power units in the $300 to $500 range, with transom-mount transducers. As I did so the observer and I communicated over FRS radio, and we watched in amazement as some fish began to avoid swimming under the boat, or speeded up to do so, when the units were active. As soon as I turned them off, the fish started going under the boat again. At one point when a unit was pinging away, a sea turtle in the tank swam up to the boat and literally bit the one transducer that was active at that moment.

I can't say exactly how these sea creatures heard, felt, or otherwise sensed the units, but I can say for sure that in one way or another it affected them. It particularly disturbed the rays and shark in the tank. There were no stripers in that particular display tank, so unfortunately I can't swear that striped bass can hear your fishfinder. But don't be so quick to accept that salesman's assurances when he says no, the fish won't hear your new fishfinder. And when stealth counts, you may want to consider shutting it off.

There are considerations other than stealth when approaching a rip, as well. The most important is boat positioning; you'll need to put yourself within casting distance of the rip's feeding zone(s), but come no closer than is necessary. The farther away you remain, the less chance of spooking the fish. Obviously, driving your boat over any part of the rip is taboo. Same goes for any shadows created by you or your boat. Fish have a built-in fear of shadows, since they may mean the approach of feathered predators from above. To get into position without blowing any of these factors, prior to approaching the rip one must decide whether to anchor or drift it. You'll have to make this call on a case-by-case basis depending on the wind and sea conditions, speed of the current, bottom type, etc. Bottom line: anchoring allows you to better focus on a single specific rip but represents a more significant time investment in that one spot, while drifting maintains your flexibility to move to other parts of the same rip or move on to a new one. In most cases, maintaining that flexibility is important and you'll be better served by dropping the anchor only when it's necessary (say, the current's cranking past a small rip and drifting allows no more than a single cast at the target,) or when you have already drifted the rip once or twice and established that it's so productive, you're willing to stay put and bank on it for the time being.

You've established your approach pattern, and quietly positioned the boat such that you can cast into the feeding zone—it's time to get hooked up. Make your first cast into or beyond the feeding zone as far as possible to one side or the other, and follow it by fan-casting through the entire feeding zone. If you get a strike or catch a fish, concentrate on that particular part of the feeding zone. No bites? Then repeat the process, allowing your lure a few seconds to sink before starting the retrieves (assuming you're not pitching topwater lures). Continue allowing it to go deeper and deeper until you're bouncing your lure across the bottom. Still no bites? Then it's time to move on.

There are two types of rips which differ from the norm, and require unique plans of attack. The first is a rip created by a point of land. In most cases, as stated earlier this will look from above more or less like half of a rip—instead of the ripples extending off to either side of the structure, a single line of ripples extends out on one side, only. In this case the parts of the rip remain essentially the same construct, but there may be one interesting note about the feeding zone: a secondary feeding zone is often created either forward of the rip and eddy, or well behind it.

When approaching a rip on a point, after working the primary feeding zone always work up the shore line in either direction for at least 50' or so. It's hard to predict which side of the eddy the secondary feeding zone will exist on, and it will change with different tides in different locations. In most cases, however, it exists on one side or the other—not both. If you work in one direction from a rip and quickly locate that second zone, and there is another point you're thinking about hitting not too far away, don't waste time by circling back to the opposite side of the first rip and looking for a third feeding zone there, because you usually won't find it. Just head right over to that next point, instead.

Interestingly, when the secondary zone exists on the down-current side of the eddy, this often seems to be the area you'll catch your largest stripers in. When casting to the main feeding zone produces a dozen fish in the 16" to 26" range, for example, the one 30"

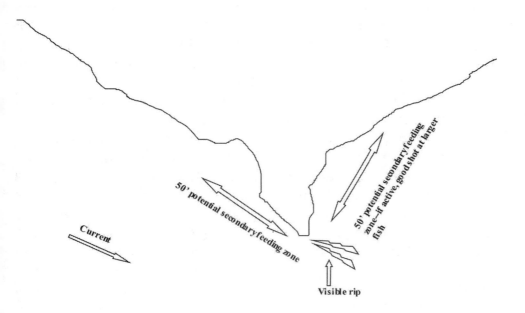

After working the primary feeding zone of a rip on a point of land, be sure to work either side and try to find a secondary feeding zone.

fish of the day may well come from down-current of the eddy, in that secondary zone.

The second oddball rip situation is when one is created by colliding currents, and there is no structure or eddy to speak of. This situation is most commonly encountered in and around inlets, and in the ocean. In either case this type of feature should always be fished on the drift, because its exact location is likely to shift constantly as the currents and tidal patterns shift. Commonly, baitfish being squeezed or confused by the colliding water is what stripers will be feeding on in rips like these, and the usual rules go out the window. Often the location of the fish will be marked by gulls which are feeding on the same baitfish or on fish that are injured in the feeding frenzy, so always keep an eye peeled for birds when working a current-to-current rip. Constantly cast around and prospect, and don't expect the fish to stay in any one place for long. If any one area of a current rip is likely to be better than the others, it's going to be the perimeter. Again, don't stick there and fish it continually if you're not catching fish. But on the initial approach try the perimeter first, before prospecting in and around the rips.

Effectively fishing in structural rips with bait is an entirely different matter than fishing them with lures. Instead of constantly casting and retrieving, you'll need to position you boat so you can toss or drift the bait into the feeding zone, using the current to your advantage. It's almost always easier to do this at anchor, though good captains working in decent conditions can hold the boat in position while his anglers get their baits into the strike zone. If, that is, they're willing to set down their fishing rod and concentrate on boat-handling. In large areas of multiple rips or in current-formed rips, many anglers will simply drift through with their baits deployed. This is effective in some places at some times, but doesn't allow you to work specific zones of specific structural rips. Use this tactic to prospect—once you locate the hotspot, you're usually better of by sticking to it and focusing your efforts in that specific location until you cease getting strikes.

What kinds of baits are effective in rips? Any that stripers like to eat, so long as they're present in the place you're fishing, at the time you're fishing. That said, most of the time stripers found in rips are feeding on baitfish. Live mullet, spot, perch, or eels can all be drifted back into a rip with great results, but peanut bunker usually have a tough time on the hook in a strong current and will probably die quickly. If you're positioned such that you need to cast, allow your bait to drift through the feeding zone, then reel in and cast again; menhaden usually won't last for more than two or three casts.

You'll need to make a few tackle adjustments when fishing with bait in rips, too. It's much harder to control what depth your offering passes through the rip at, and in most cases you'll be limited to fishing it at the surface, or on the bottom. If you can identify areas where the fish are feeding high in the water column, fine; live-line or freespool your baits, and let them enter the feeding zone at the surface. If the fish are feeding sub-surface, however, you'll need to choose between your weight options depending on how and where your boat is positioned. Remember: the ultimate goal is to put that bait into the feeding zone. If you're rigged up with a bank sinker, egg sinker, or torpedo weight, you'll have to consider the fact that any significant amount of current will roll these weights along the bottom. Accordingly, don't cast for the middle of the feeding zone because by the time your rig sinks down to the bottom it may well have washed right out of the good area. Instead, cast well up-current so that when your weight does roll along the bottom, it carries your bait through the best part of the rip.

Since rips are formed by moving water, the only way to fish a bait in one and hope to have it stay in place is to use a pyramid weight, which is designed to hold bottom in a crashing surf. Unfortunately, this is problematic because quite often whatever structure the rip forms around will foul your sinker, and you'll lose the entire rig.
There is one better way to attempt to position a bait in a rip, if conditions allow. If the captain can hold the boat up-current of the rip and the angler can cast directly into the eddy or simply drift it back, the bait will have a few seconds of sink-time before the current grabs the line and pulls it along. If the boat position is maintained, the angler can sometimes get his bait to pass right through the strike zone, sim-

ply by keeping his line taunt and dropping back intermittently as the moving water picks the weight up off the bottom.

Scours

Another great feeding condition for striped bass which is caused by tidal currents are scours. These are holes and undercuts in banks or the bottom, where time and moving water has eaten out sediments and caused an overhang. Many of the Jersey and New York sod banks have scours, as do cuts running between marsh islands in the Chesapeake. Often scours occur on the outside of channel bends, and are opposite underwater points.

Undercuts can be fished with either baits or lures but since

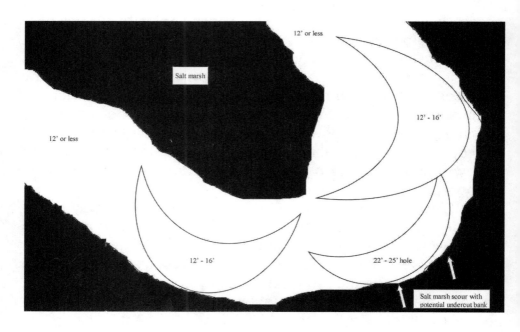

Scours form on the outside of bends. The water will often be twice or even three times the depth of the surrounding areas, and the bank may be undercut.

these are areas where the current flows in one direction or the other more or less all the time, it's another situation in which bait fishing is usually tough. You'll face the same problem of rolling weights and snags. That's not to say it can't be done effectively, but for the most part scours are best fished with lures.

When casting to a scour you'll usually want to cast as close as possible to the undercut, allow your bait or lure to sink (if necessary), and retrieve along the shoreline if at all possible. In many cases, that may mean positioning your boat within a few feet of land just up-current of the scour, and casting more or less parallel to the bank. Once you've worked a section thoroughly, move the boat 20' or 30' down the bank and continue casting.

Slow-trolling with light tackle is another way to work a scour. This method works best when the entire feature is flanked by shallow, muddy bottom, and the bank is not undercut. It also allows you to work a number of scours in quick succession, if you're fishing along a series of them in a winding, twisting marsh cut. On those occasions when the tide dies out it may also be possible to vertical jig in scours. Unfortunately, often when this is the case the fish aren't feeding very hard, anyway. Still, keep it in mind for that window of the tidal frame if the fish are holding in the bottom of the deepest section and are still willing to bite. In this situation metal usually works best. Stingsilvers, Hopkins, and similar lures should do the trick.

Tide and Fish Behavior

For the most part, thus far we've focused on the physical effects of the tides and currents, and how they create situations which are conducive to holding fish. But the greatest effect of the tides is upon the fish themselves. Rockfish are particularly tidal-sensitive, and any striper angler worth his salt knows that as often as not the tides dictate the fish's behavior regardless of the physical surroundings.

This will change from place to place and situation to situation, but as a general rule of thumb note that stripers will usually feed during the last hour or so of one tidal cycle and/or the first hour or so of the next tidal cycle. Sometimes they'll feed right through the change, sometimes they'll favor one period over the other, and often they'll feed until the tide stops moving, take a rest, then start up again when the current resumes its motion. Sometimes the fish will fall into feeding patterns revolving around the tide which may last for a couple of weeks, a month, or even an entire season. They may favor the incoming, or it may be the outgoing—and the next week or month or season, the opposite could be true. If you're like me, you can pretty much plan on the fish shifting their pattern right about the time you finally have it figured out.

Quite often, it'll be the incoming that's hot in one particular area but the outgoing in another. In the surf up and down the coast, for example, the last of the incoming is generally the best bite. Sometimes this won't be true and some seasons it will be wrong more than it's right. But if you look over the long haul and smooth out the anomalies with time, the last of the incoming is probably the best part of the tide to fish in the surf sixty or seventy percent of the time. Yet in the bays, where cuts and creeks drain from the marshes, the same could be said for the first of the outgoing tide. Here, stripers will pick off baitfish and crustaceans as they're washed out of the marsh, and the falling tide favors their hunting technique. In open water, it really is a toss up. In fact, it's even harder to predict what portion of the tidal cycle the fish will feed best on, since they have so many different feeding options.

If you're not catching fish during a particular section of the tidal cycle, don't just sit there and wait for it to change—go on the hunt. Quite often, a chumming bite will die off with a tidal change. But jigging spoons, soft-plastics, or feather jigs worked through the same area will stimulate the bite that seemed to disappear. Again speaking generally, the catching during an off-tide does seem best when you're fishing in a way that creates a reaction strike—surface poppers will draw more bites than a dead chunk of bait; shad-tail plastics and twister tails will draw more than straight tail plastics or bucktails; and an erratic retrieve out-produces a steady one during this time frame.

Just how important is it to consider the effect of the tide on rockfish? Over a decade ago, I got a program for my computer called Tides and Currents. This program allowed me to put a 24-hour period of the tide into a bar-graph format. Since the spring trophy season had just reopened after a closed season that lasted for years, I decided to greet the rejuvenated fishery with healthy enthusiasm and vigor. I pulled out all the stops, tried just about everything in the books (and a lot of things that aren't in any book, except this one or

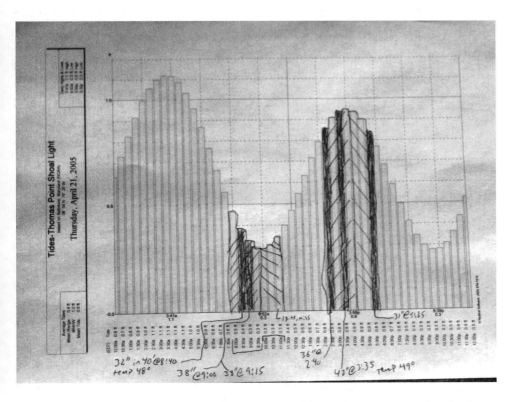

A marked print-out from Tides and Currents, documenting bait-caught trophy stripers in the Chesapeake Bay.

Rudow's Guide to Fishing the Chesapeake!) and kept track of each and every trophy caught on my boat and my father's boat. Take note: only the fish caught on bait, using the tactics outlined in chapter 10 for spring trophy chumming, were recorded. This data represents this type of fishing only, and has no relevance whatsoever to fish caught while trolling. Whenever I could confirm a catch by a friend and had verifiable data on it including the date, the exact time of the catch, water temperature, depth, clarity, and fish size, I documented it as well. All of these trophy stripers were documented by printing out one of the Tides and Currents bar graphs for that particular day, and marking the tidal bar in the graph which corresponded to the time the fish was caught.

Five years later, flipping through the print-outs, certain patterns became crystal clear. Approximately 80-percent of the trophies were caught in a one and a half hour window of the tide, occurring twice a day: the last 90 minutes of the tidal cycle. Another 10 percent came during the next hour, which included about 30 minutes of dead tide and the first 30 minutes of the next tide. The remaining oddball 10-percent were caught at sunrise or sunset during ambient light, regardless of the tidal cycle.

Eliminating the sunrise/sunset bites from the mix—as stated earlier, this time period is often utilized by the fish for feeding regardless of other factors—and all of the bait-caught trophies were caught during a two and a half hour stretch of the tide. After another five seasons, there were still no exceptions to the 80-percent/10-percent/10-percent pattern. A full decade of data proves it beyond any doubt. During some specific seasons more of the bites came earlier in the period, and during other seasons more came later. One year the incoming would be the most productive, and the next the outgoing might be the better cycle. But the vast majority of the catches continued to fall in the hot 90-minute sliver of the tidal cycle, with a few fish coming at the other specified times.

In other specific fisheries, the tidal influence is usually not this dramatic. In fact, I know of no other situation where it seems so incredibly carved in stone, with the possible exception of the winter inlet eeling bite for stripers in North Carolina. (I haven't documented enough time in these inlets to prove the matter, but it sure seems that way!) But this example offers great insight into just how huge the influence of tide can be when it comes to fishing for striped bass.

Now, are we ready to drop the other shoe? They say there are no absolutes in fishing, and whoever the heck "they" are, they're right. During the winter and spring of 2005/2006 I did a lot of speaking engagements at boat shows, conventions and sportfishing group meetings, to promote my book Rudow's Guide to Fishing the Chesapeake. Often, I would hand out print-outs from Tides and Currents, and explain the findings with great confidence—after all, I had over a decade of documentation including literally hundreds of catches, backing up my assertions. For some reason, maybe just to make a fool out of me, that spring the fish shifted their pattern. Nearly half of the trophies we caught were in the hour following the normal "hot" part of the cycle (when only 10-percent of them should have been caught). They still established a feeding cycle dictated by the tides and it wasn't too terribly far off from the norm (50-40 versus 80-10,) but if I hadn't documented it myself I never would have believed it— the fish deviated from a decade-old pattern which was evidenced as well as any in the world of recreational fishing. Go figure...

The lesson we anglers must take from this experience? You can pattern the fish and use your acquired knowledge to hunt them more effectively. But no matter what you discover, never ever say never.

Established Tidal Patterns

If I were a better record keeper, I'd be able to list out every striper caught with every method during every cycle of the tide. Unfortunately, that would take a huge effort and I don't know anyone who's ever done it. (If you do, give me a call—boy, would I like to get my hands on that data!) However, through the years some other generalized patterns have made themselves clear. They are not as exact as the spring trophy patterns identified earlier and they will fluctuate quite a bit, but at least in my mind, these are fairly good generalizations which I use to be a more effective angler. Put them into play, and I'll bet you'll become a more effective angler, too.

One final caution: these rules of thumb can be used to enhance your fishing, but should not regulate it. I must again stress: there are no absolutes when it comes to fishing, and you will encounter situations when the confluence of other factors—light levels, weather patterns, etc.—overwhelms the tidal influence and these rules will go out the window. I include these here as loose guidelines of general striper feeding behavior relating to the tide.

• Migrating spring fish, chumming/bait chunks – Very rigid patterns, adhering to the last hour of one tide and the first hour of the next tide.

• Migrating spring fish, trolling – Rigid patterns but with a wider window; usually the last two and a half hours of one tide into the first hour of the next tide.

• School/local fish, chumming/bait – The peak hour to two hours of the tide with the strongest current, with an increase in activity when the tide begins to fall. The increased action usually lasts for half an hour or so, or until the tide slacks. Shortly after or during the switch of the tide is also productive at times.

• School/local fish, trolling – Varies greatly from season to season with the best action usually taking place some time around the peak current strength. Shortly after or during the switch of the tide is also productive at times.

• School/local fish, jigging or caught while breaking water – All bets are off; the presence of schooled bait and sometimes light levels seems to have as much or more effect on when this type of feeding/fishing is active than tidal cycles do.

• Eeling – Usually the last hour before the end of a tide. Sometimes during the absolutely dead tide. Note—many seasons the eeling bite will either be on or off, with no in-between, during each particular slice of the tide. If you're eeling and the bite dies out it's usually wise to switch your fishing method completely.

• Surf Fishing – The last two hours of an incoming tide and/or the first hour of an outgoing tide.

• Casting to rips – The two hour portion of the tidal cycle with peak current flow in the area you're fishing. The switch of the tide also brings bites.

• Casting to marsh/tidal creek mouths – The first two hours of the outgoing tide.

• Casting to rip-rap, points, and other shallow-water features – Light levels trump tidal cycle. That said, high water is generally better than low water. When sunrise coincides with peak high tide, conditions are optimal.

• Fishing inlet jetties – The last hour and a half of each tidal cycle. Shortly after or during the switch of the tide is also productive at times.

• Fishing color/temp breaks just outside of inlets – the latter half of the outgoing tide.

• Night fishing – Varies greatly; may establish a pattern around any specific slice of the tide but tends to depend more upon light levels and moon phase.

Note that for all of the above situations and techniques, generally speaking the times of peak feeding will grow longer in the fall. Just when this begins to happen depends on your exact location along the coast; it may start in September in northern areas, and it may start as late as November in southern areas. Each season it will vary, depending upon other conditions.

CHAPTER THREE

WEATHER SYSTEM CHANGES AND SEASONAL CHANGES

The tactics of a successful striper angler will vary radically, from one to another.

You're anchored up on a shoal, and the chumming bite is slow but steady. You can see a front approaching in the distance. As it moves closer the bite picks up. As the front moves overhead the fish go crazy—as soon as you get a bait in the water it gets hit, and the catching is fast and furious for several minutes. Then, when the front passes, the fish shut down like someone flipped a switch. What the heck is going on?

There's great debate about the effects of weather systems and pressure changes in the world of fishing. Exactly what causes the fish to feed hard or not at all? No one knows for sure, but there's no doubt that these influences have a huge effect on the fish. Traditionally, most people have believed the pressure changes accompanying weather systems are the defining factor. There's just one problem with this theory: remember that way back in high-school, they taught you that water can't be compressed? And the fish are below the water's surface. Thus, the actual physical impact on the fish due to pressure changes should be minimal at best and possibly even undetectable by the fish. In fact, science points to less and less of a potential influence due to pressure changes, the deeper you dig. Consider hydrostatic pressure, for example. Water has 800 times the density of air. By merely swimming up or down by three feet, the fish have undergone a pressure change (a tenth of an atmosphere; 33 feet underwater doubles the atmospheric pressure) that is significantly greater and more rapidly than a massive weather event, such as a hurricane. Now consider waves. A three-foot wave passing over a fish has the same effect, as rapidly as the wave is traveling. Considering these factors, how could a measly little barometric change affect the fish? Who knows—but it does, or at least something connected with it does.

As pressure drops, fishing often picks up in the shallows and fish are more likely to strike topwater baits. As it rises, they often go deep. If the barometer rises to an extreme—say, over 30.5—the fish often go to the bottom and appear to sit there. And yet the changes created by that moving barometer are likely to be as little as 0.02 per hour for a slow moving front, or 0.05 per hour for a fast moving storm.

Whatever the scientific reasons are for the striped bass's behavior, the bottom line is that we must consider it in order to boost our catch. Remember that a slow change in the barometer is best for a long day of fishing, while abrupt changes are likely to trigger short-lived but extreme feeding frenzies. Try to time your fishing efforts prior to a front hitting, and fish through the event. If the fish shut down, expect them to remain inactive for at least several hours. On some occasions, they'll remain inactive for the rest of the day and may not pick up to their original activity level until the next morning.

Of course, when a front passes through the results are not always so dramatic. Sometimes they'll continue feeding, albeit with reduced vigor. Note that many times if you keep a close eye on the fishfinder, you'll see that fish which were near the surface or were suspended at mid depth prior to the front's passing will drop down to the bottom and hug it. Expect that even when the fish do continue to feed after such an event you may need to change tactics accordingly, to keep your offering near the fish.

Extremely large storms such as hurricanes often have the same effect, on a much larger scale. When there's a day of calm before the storm, rockfish will often feed like nuts. In fact, just prior to a storm of significance there's often a period of light winds and sunshine during which the bite is excellent. There's a hurricane on its way up the coast? The day before it's scheduled to hit in your neck of the woods, take off work and grab your fishing rods. Naturally, it should also be noted that you must plan on being back at the dock well in advance of the initial effects of such a storm; if it's supposed to arrive in 10 or 12 hours, you're already too late to go fishing—only take advantage of this situation a full day before the arrival of the storm.

Another effect the weather has is on light levels. We've discussed the importance of this factor elsewhere in this book but it bears repeating the fact that incoming weather with heavy cloud cover can encourage the bite, and breaking from cloud cover to sunny weather often suppresses it. Rain in and of itself does not appear to have a dramatic impact on the fish unless it's strong enough to create muddy flow from rivers and tributaries, discoloring the water. Usually, in most tidal areas that sort of impact won't be felt until a day or two after the rain falls, in any case. But there are two more aspects to rainfall that are important to keep in mind: the first is that it drives away your competition, and in areas of heavy boat traffic, this can have a notable positive effect. A steady rain that is not accompanied by heavy winds or rough seas should be welcomed by die-hard anglers with open arms. Many other fishermen will stay at home, cruisers will remain in port, and fish that are driven down by prop whines and constant traffic will go into feeding mode. Utilize these conditions to your best advantage by hitting high-pressure fishing zones. Spots that are widely known by even the most amateurish anglers, yet get so much pressure that they're avoided by dedicated fishermen, can become prime targets when it's pouring. Get yourself some quality foul weather gear, and instead of canceling your fishing plans when it rains, get excited.

The second impact of note is that driving rain which is not accompanied by heavy winds will flatten out the seas. Although this may not directly impact the fish it does give you the opportunity to spot visible rips more effectively than in clear but windy conditions. When a downpour turns the bay slick-calm, suddenly those ripples which were obscured by wind-driven waves will become obvious. If you're having trouble deciding whether to fish open water or inshore rips and it's a rainy, windless day, this may tip the scales and make your decision a little easier.

The winds will also have an effect on the fish's feeding mode, especially if you're fishing in relatively shallow water. More specifically, it's the wind-driven currents that have the impact you're most interested in. A steady wind will push bait up against structure, where it may then become confused and panicked. When there's a wind out of the south, for example, southern points or rip-rapped shorelines which are being pounded by the waves are more likely to hold actively feeding fish than points or rip-rap on the north side of the structure. Before you file that one away in the brain, note the flip-side of the equation: if the wind's too strong and the waves smacking the shore are violent, it may turn the water cloudy and force the fish to feed elsewhere. For this reason, depending on the bottom type, a moderate breeze is generally better than a honkin' wind when you're attacking the windward side of a shoreline.

Underwater ridges and humps as much as five or six feet below the surface can be affected in the same way. Much deeper than this the waves won't have any real impact, but so long as that wind-driven current smacks into something, there's the possibility baitfish will be trapped up against it. So in a perfect world, that 10- to 15-mph breeze would drive relatively small waves to hit the hotspot—but would never turn into a 20-mph breeze and three-foot waves.

When you're fishing the shallows, don't let discolored water discourage you too quickly. Remember those big eyes—stripers can see and attack baitfish in water much dirtier than one might think. Unless the water is absolute mud, try a few casts to a couple of hotspots, before giving up hope in the shallows.

When the wind-driven waves have murked up the water to the point that it's impossible to fish, there is one more way you can use the conditions to your advantage: look for winding creeks and cuts which drain marshes, particularly towards the latter half of the falling tide. Although many shallow water spots will be tough to access as water levels drop, once the churned up water that flowed into the marsh during the incoming tide has more or less been expelled, you'll often discover a plume of clean water flowing out of the marsh. The stripers know where and when to look for this improved clarity, too, and they'll be there at the mouth of the creek, ready to eat.

What about rough versus calm seas in open water? There may in fact be an impact upon the striper's behavior depending on the nature of these conditions, but if there is one, I don't know of anyone who's documented it and I haven't observed any direct correlations myself. That said, trolling catches do seem to be enhanced at times due to rough weather. This is likely a function of the seas' effect on your boat—as it's rocked this way and rolled that way, it imparts a natural jigging action on your lures which makes them appear more life-like than the steady action created by a slow-moving, stable boat.

Unfortunately, rough seas often have the opposite effect on chummers. The constant motion jerks rods up and down, and the fish feel intermittent resistance on the line when they grab a chunk bait. You can mitigate the effect by holding your rod in your hand and keeping it steady as the boat rocks, but when the waves are really big, you may find trolling is the more effective tactic.

Surf fishermen should also be attuned to the winds. When they roar down the coast from the northeast they may well churn the surf into un-fishable towering waves and white froth. Naturally, this is the day you should pick to stay at home. The first calm following a blow, however, can be extremely productive. Clams, sand fleas, and crabs get ripped up and pounded in the rough surf, and as soon as that wind eases the stripers will often go into feeding mode. This is a good time to match the hatch; fish with clams, calico crab chunks, soft sand fleas, or bloodworms.

The final weather effect striper anglers should pay attention to is sudden temperature changes. Of course, these are usually accompanied by frontal boundaries and pressure changes, but it's the delayed effect we're looking for here. It will occur most significantly in the fall, with the exact timing depending on your location on the coast. When the first abrupt cold snap of the fall hits and air temperatures drop down a good 20-degrees overnight, stripers will often jump into feeding mode. This is not always an instantaneous phenomenon; it may take a couple of days before the fish really kick it into high gear. But often, in the week following an abrupt fall temperature plunge, stripers will be seen feeding much more actively. Finding the fish up top breaking water becomes a lot more common, and active feeding periods of the tidal cycle are suddenly extended. The fish school up rapidly, and while you were seeing scattered patches of fish prior to the temperature shift, suddenly those patches come together to form massive, tightly-packed schools.

Naturally, the warm-up in late spring and early summer also has an effect. Unfortunately, for anglers in the southern end of the striper's range it's the opposite of the fall effect, and as temperatures rise to summer levels the stripers will usually go into dog-days mode. Feeding becomes lackluster during daylight hours, the stripers tend to hold deeper to find cooler water temperatures, and surface action becomes nonexistent in southern areas. But, there are still plenty of ways to catch fish during the dog days—more on that later. And for anglers in the northern range, the rising temperatures are a good thing, until the mercury starts rising beyond the comfort range.

Seasonal Changes – Early Spring

Seasonal changes have a huge impact on the way rockfish feed. Early spring means spawning fish, and mature stripers will be on the move. In many areas the fishery remains closed, and in some others harvest is strictly regulated or only catch and release fishing is allowed. In northern areas the fish simply aren't in town yet, and in coastal areas there aren't many fish around because they've all headed up-river or up a bay, returning to their freshwater birthplace. Most years, stripers will have minimal interest in feeding as they head for their spawning grounds. March and April are spent with reproduction in mind. Yes, the fish will eat—but it's not their main concern. The fish are traveling in small pods or alone, and even the "schoolie" fish haven't schooled up yet. These are some of the reasons (though not the main one; more on that later) why trolling tends to be more effective than chumming or bait fishing; the motion of a trolled lure may cause a reaction strike during a wider range of the tidal cycle than bait, which is more or less eaten out of convenience. Meanwhile, the fish won't hold in a chum slick, but will quickly return to their migration route after a brief investigation.

Interestingly, during this time frame the pre-spawn fish will often more or less ignore live baits. Fishing live herring in the pre-spawn season, for example, you'll usually get fewer strikes than you will if you use cut baits. Perhaps this is because the fish want to expend as little energy as possible, or maybe they don't want to get preoccupied with

This striper was taken off Thomas Point, under a balloon, on the off period of the tide for chumming.

chasing down a baitfish while they have other goals in mind. I don't believe anyone knows the true answer to this question. But whatever it may be, the fact that you must bear in mind to increase your fishing effectiveness remains the same: cut dead baits usually out-produce live baitfish when you're targeting large pre-spawn fish on their way to the breeding grounds.

These pre-spawn migrators spend most of their time high in the water column. Even when they travel through water 100' deep, most will be caught within 30' of the surface and a great number will be caught just 10' to 20' below the surface. Trollers fishing in the early spring are best served by setting most of their lines to run accordingly. Bait fishermen, meanwhile, will discover that for some reasons (try and figure out a reasonable explanation for this one!) baits set in the upper water column will largely go ignored. Instead, baits set dead on the bottom in 20' to 50' depths will take the majority of their strikes. Perhaps the fish drop down to the bottom during that small slice of the tidal cycle during which they can be bait-caught in the early spring, or maybe that's just the one time when they will allow their migration to be interrupted by the scent of free food. Whatever the reason, take note of this fact and you'll catch more fish.

There is one exception, which will be explored in more detail later on in chapter 7: whole rigged dead menhaden suspended in the upper water column to look like they are mortally injured will take some rockfish shortly before and shortly after the usual "hot" slice of the tide for bait fishing.

Seasonal Changes
Late Spring/Early Summer

As spring progresses more areas become open to recreational fishing, and post-spawn fish become more and more common. Since the spawn is fairly spread out in most areas, from early April through early May many rivers and bays will see a mix of pre- and post-spawn stripers. By mid-May most seasons (weather patterns will have an effect) the spawn is more or less over. The migratory fish begin their trek up the coast, while school-sized fish move into open water and begin grouping up.

During this time frame, in southern areas chumming tends to grow in effectiveness as trolling drops off a bit. Jigging fish in open water becomes possible but tough—most of the schools are still small and fairly scattered. Meanwhile, trolling tops the list in northern states. Pulling umbrellas, spoons and large lipped plugs becomes commonplace. The fish get more and more active and catches pick up, usually into the month of June.

Early summer in the southern areas of the rockfish's range is a toss-up: some years there's a good bite on large adults that decided to hang around for a while before scooting up the coast, and some other years the big fish cruise and the school fish haven't schooled up yet. The bite in northern areas, meanwhile, usually continues getting better and better. This is a time of transition for all areas, but the good fishing seen in the Chesapeake region will usually drop off by the end of the month as the same stripers they were catching move up the coast to the delight of New Jersey and New York anglers. Other stocks of fish are pouring out of the Hudson and similar northern breeding grounds adding to the northern bite, whereas southern anglers won't ever get a shot at these fish. For some the summer doldrums have already arrived and a lot of time will be spent prospecting and trying different tactics, while for others, prime spring angling is still in full swing.

Seasonal Changes
Summer

Summer usually brings a slow period to the striper's southern range. From New Jersey south the water temperatures have probably risen above the fish's preferred 80-degree upper threshold of comfort. Striped bass will, at this point, go deep. Depth means cooler water temperatures, and if you can spot a thermocline you may well find the magic depth to fish at.

On the Chesapeake Bay, at this time of year anglers will face another tough challenge: dealing with the dead zone. The dead zone is an area of anoxic (oxygen-free) water which can not support life. It usually forms in water at least 30' deep, and may stretch from the upper bay all the way down to its mouth.

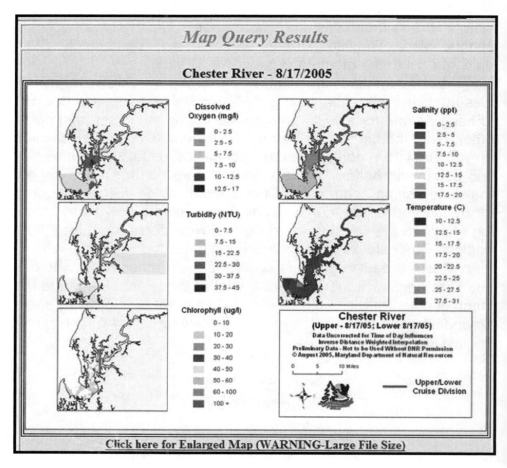

Check the web before fishing during the warm months of the year when dead zones pop up; the different shading seen here is in color on-screen, and you'll be able to locate the depths and areas of low oxygen water.

The fish, meanwhile, are trying to get down deep to where it's cool. Obviously, they can't hang out in the dead zone. So a key feature Chesapeake anglers need to identify from June through September is the location of the dead zone. Savvy anglers will target the five or 10' immediately above the dead water, wherever structure may intersect with this particular depth. It's easy to figure out just where the bad water starts—often you can tell because you won't see a single fish mark on your depth finder below a specific point. But prior to fishing you can identify the depths of the dead zone and put together a coherent, effective game plan that will help you out-fish the competition by going to http://mddnr.chesapeakebay.net/eyeson-thebay/index.cfm. This web site has water quality charting that will clearly show you where the dead zone is, and how bad it is. This site is also useful after periods of heavy rain, because you can also find satellite shots showing water turbidity and salinity. It will help you ascertain how far to run, where to launch, and how to plan to find clean water.

During this time frame night fishing becomes significantly more effective than fishing during broad daylight. Until the water cools with the change of the seasons, the stripers will feed individually after the sun is down, often along bridge light-lines and under other artificial light sources. They'll establish this pattern on the southern end of the range first, but by August this is usually true of rockfish pretty much wherever you find them. That's not to say you won't catch any during the day—you certainly will. But when the fish are reported to be in a summer slump, it's often simply because they're doing their eating at night, when there are fewer people targeting them.

Seasonal Changes
Fall/Early Winter

Fall is, without question, the best season for striper anglers in most areas. The fish feed and they feed hard, trying to fatten up before winter sets in. Breaking water on bay anchovies, glass minnow, sand eels, and bunker becomes common. The fish in open water gather together into tight schools (making them easier to target,) and good numbers of fish continue to feed in the shallows of coastal bays and tributaries.

As one would expect, the bulk of the striped bass begin migrating back down the coast when the cool fall temperatures kick in. Interestingly, however, the fall migration is not as long and drawn out

Fall chumming means fast action...

as one might think. Sure, some of the fish will depart northern climes as early as September, while others will wait for one or even two more months before they head south. But the bulk of the fish will feed strongly well into November, before turning tail and heading south. Once the fish start migrating in earnest, they'll be hundreds of miles south in a matter of weeks.

Meanwhile, resident fish are putting on the feed bag. By mid October or early November, the fish's peak feeding times have expanded greatly and may well be double what they were a few months ago. Many northern anglers have already pulled their boats at this point—a tragedy!—and only the die-hards are left on the water. Too bad for everyone else. Those of us who still have full access to the water at this point will often experience the best topwater action of

...and big smiles.

the year, as this is the time when the stripers are most likely to be found busting bait on the surface. Just about any tactic works well, as the fish feed with abandon. Thanksgiving often marks the best of the late season fishing in the middle of the striper's range, though up north it may be more or less over by this point. During the 2006 season the opposite was true. Thanks to ridiculously high temperatures the fish didn't move south until very late in the year, and the bulk of the schools of fish weren't south of Delaware until near Christmas. Of course, this season was an oddball—let's hope global warming doesn't make it a regular event.

Soon, the chill that sparked the fish into action will become downright cold. The fish slow down and the sight of bass busting water will become a rare one, once again. As winter sets in, however, there's often a good shallow water bite. Many residential fish will move into river mouths and inlets in preparation for the winter, and can be caught by casting light tackle in shallow water well into December. Plan on this action starting up as the water drops into the 50's and it will continue until the water drops into the 40's. In most areas these will be a relatively small class of fish, consisting mostly of stripers under 30". The big fish, meanwhile, are holding in big schools off the coast. Early in December in southern areas of the range it's often still possible to get into these fish as they churn the surface or by drifting eels over the near-shore shoals (as long as most of the blues have departed—-if not, you'll need lots of eels,) but at some point their activity level drops with the temperature and trolling heavy gear becomes the most effective way to take these fish. During this time frame, Cape Charles, Rudee Inlet, Oregon Inlet, and Cape Fear will produce excellent catches of fish in the 30" to 50" class.

CHAPTER FOUR

SHALLOW WATER LIGHT-TACKLE STRIPER FISHING
A tactical approach

The best thing any angler can do to learn how to fish the shallows effectively is to have his boat break down, and be forced to spend a season with a small jon boat. (I'm assuming most of you have a back-up boat. If you don't, you should get one immediately. No striper angler's home is complete without a jon boat in the back yard.) Being stuck with a little 14' aluminum job and a 10-hp. motor really forces you to focus on the water that's close to home, in tributary rivers and creeks, inside inlets, and protected coves. And if you're ever stuck with a little boat like this for a season, you'll be amazed when you look back at how many fish you caught on it. Fish the shallows effectively, and there will be plenty of days on which you come home with more, bigger fish than the guys who fished out in the deep.

Of course, if you're interested in sheer numbers of fish caught, you can't limit yourself to just one kind of fishing. But numbers alone are not the main reason why people like fishing the shallows. It's the ability to hook into big fish on light gear that attracts most of us to the tactic.

You can employ shallow water casting tackle and tactics in just about any body of water at just about any time. No matter whether you're fishing Buzzards Bay or Albemarle Sound, there will be shallow water structure somewhere around you. Rip-rapped shorelines, points, underwater bars, rockpiles, bridge pilings, creek mouths, docks, pound nets, and banks all provide you with a target. Generally speaking, spots like these which are hit by some form of current are better than those that aren't, and if they form rips, even better. When you work a shoreline, you're best served by moving the boat with an electric motor or a four-stroke motor at idle, slowly putting along from visible structure to visible structure, shifting into neutral and cast-

Casting lures in shallow water is an exciting way to tie into energetic stripers on extremely light gear.

ing a few times at each likely looking spot. When you catch a fish or two, work the area more thoroughly. But overall, remember that if you keep moving and searching until you know a particular area well, you'll tend to do better than if you cast to the same small area over and over. Fish a shoreline three or four times and you'll discover which spots are hot and which aren't, and can stop putting so much time into exploration and do more running directly from hotspot to hotspot. In my home river, for example, the South on the middle Chesapeake Bay, the first year I moved into the area my Mercury tower-of-power blew out, leaving me with a 150-hp anchor attached to the shell of a boat. It was well beyond repair. Luckily, I had a small two-seater with a four-horse Yamaha on the transom. I spent the entire season working close to home, on the shorelines. Soon I had a new boat, but since discovering excellent fishing right in the river, I tended to cast to the shorelines quite often, especially on short pre-work fishing trips. By my third or fourth season on the river I had a dozen or so hotspots pegged, and would run from one to the next, so as to not burn up the best bite times of the day searching fruitless waters.

Surprisingly, I did discover that even the best hotspots come and go. Any particular one may be red hot one year and dead the next. And the next. Then suddenly, like someone flipped a switch, it might be full of fish again. So gather your list of favorite shallow water spots but constantly try new and different places that look good, and you'll find that they change and rotate as time goes on.

Timing your attack on the shallow water spots is fairly simple: most seasons in most places, shallow water fishing is best at sunrise and sunset. Of course, some days the bite goes on continually and some others it never materializes. So if there's a full day of fishing ahead, you may want to plan on hitting shallow water hotspots X, Y, and Z, which are on the way to trolling spot A or chumming spot B in deeper water. If the fish keep hitting as the day progresses, great— keep banging on them in the shallows. But if they stop striking once the sun's been up for and hour or two, shift gears and head for your planned deepwater spot. If you base your game plan on several different types of fishing which allow you to try several different areas and depths throughout the day, you'll end up catching a whole lot more fish than the inflexible captain who decides to do one thing, period. Maintaining this flexibility not only helps you catch more fish, it also keeps your anglers happy. Doing one thing all day long, be it trolling or throwing lures over and over ad infinitum, can become boring for just about anyone. There's only one down-side to this approach: you'll have to haul along two or three different rod and reel set-ups for every angler you plan to have aboard.

Tackle

Just how light can shallow water casting gear go? For tossing lures up to rip-rap, points and cuts, most people will use a six and a half or seven foot medium-action rod in the 10 to 12 pound class, either spinning or casting, spooled up with monofilament. And in most cases, they're over-gunned for the circumstances. Instead, try throwing a six-foot light/fast action rod such as a St. Croix SCII or a six and a half foot Falcon SSti 66M with a reel spooled up with 12 pound test, four pound diameter Berkeley Fireline or Power Pro. No, I don't get kickbacks or free gear from either of these companies, but I'm not afraid of naming names, either. I use this stuff on a daily basis, and I'll bet dollars to doughnuts you'll catch more fish using this variety of line on this type of rod in this type of situation. Why? Because the incredibly thin diameter of this line lets you throw it a country mile—every bit as far as that longer medium-action rod spooled with 10 pound mono. But with the shorter rod, fast action, and no-stretch line, you'll be able to set the hook instantly whenever fish strike at your lure. The shorter rod is also advantageous when there are several people casting aboard a single boat, and swinging the rod gets dangerous. You'll have fewer break-offs using this gear (often you can even bend the hook out of snags, when using superlines like these) and you'll be able to cast lures as light as one quarter of an ounce, with no problem.

The reel you choose for light tackle casting can be either spinning or conventional, as you choose. An experienced caster will usually get better accuracy out of conventional gear, but no matter how good you may be, you'll pay for it with the backlash factor. In either case, be sure to pick out a make and model which has a smooth drag. If you plan on jigging with this rig as well as casting, an infinite anti-reverse feature is a must-have to prevent slap-back and maintain fast hook-sets. Line capacity is not a huge issue, since you won't usually be dropping to great depths or trailing the lure or bait far behind your boat. Finally, when it comes to reels don't go cheap. Most of the inexpensive versions out there won't stand up to saltwater use, and have jerky, hard to adjust drags. If you're not spending at least $75 or $80 on your reel, be suspicious. Some of my favorites for this type of fishing include the Penn 4300SS and the Shimano Sustain SA1000.

Lures for shallow water casting can vary widely. Many anglers prefer topwater lures, and there's no doubt these provide the most fantastic adrenalin rush when a striper blows up on the lure. They are not, however, as effective as sub-surface lures in most situations. Light spoons in silver or gold will usually produce more strikes and can be fished in all conditions; heavy, solid spoons intended for jigging will snag and break off often in the shallows. Generally speaking match the spoon color with the water color. In dark or tannic stained waters gold usually produces best, and at the other end of the spectrum, in gin-clear water silver is the natural choice. Swimming plugs are also effective at times. Those with rattles, like the Rat-L-Trap, often run hot or cold. Some days these lures out-fish all others, and on different days they go more or less untouched as different choices work out far better. Where's the pattern here? Usually, the rattles work best in discolored or muddy conditions, but there's no denying that sometimes they produce in just about any condition you can imagine. Use them as the weapon of choice when your go-to lures don't produce immediately, or give them an early shot if you feel so inclined, but if you go bite-less then don't hesitate to swap it out for a different style of lure. It should also be noted that on the days when fish don't seem to want rattlers, the use of these lures can absolutely kill the bite in any particular spot. Sometimes you'll get plenty of strikes fishing a different lure, switch to a rattler, and it completely ends the action. Other types of swimming plugs, like lipped lures such as Rapalas, do the trick from time to time. These are particularly effective when the fish are holding at the base of rip-rap, and sinking jigs or spoons get snagged as often as they get bit. Keep track of which lipped plugs run at which depths, and when the fish are holding on the rocks at four to six feet, for example, try casting a lipped plug that runs at that depth range. These can work out really well when you position yourself to cast parallel to the rocks, and can keep that plug in the strike zone at all times. Prop-baits and spinner baits are also effective at times. Yes, those funny looking lures designed for largemouth bass will draw plenty of strikes from striped bass. On occasion, they'll be the hot pick of the day. There's no distinguishable pattern I know of here, but keep a few in the box and when other things aren't working to your expectations give them a quick try.

So—which one of these lures should be your go-to lure, the first pick of the day on nearly every fishing trip? None of them. That honor is reserved for soft plastics, rigged on lead jig heads. Most of the time in the broadest of terms, you'll catch more fish casting soft plastic jigs than any of these other lures. The first reason is your ability to control depth. In relatively calm conditions a half-ounce lead-head can be used to effectively fish 15' of the water column, using the count-down method. (Give it a second to fall for every foot of depth you want; this will vary slightly depending on the type of tail you use, but you can figure out pretty quickly what number you need to count to in order to let that lure fall into the strike zone.) Compare this to zero depth control with a surface lure, and little to no control with a swimming plug or diver.

The second reason is your ability to quickly and painlessly swap out colors, patterns, and tail types. With a half-ounce jig head rigged on the above described gear, you can try 10 different colors in 10 casts without ever having to take time to cut off and re-tie your lure. Just rip off the plastic tail, and thread a new one on. This is an incredible advantage which can't be stressed enough. You'll get in three or four casts and make two or three color changes, while someone tying on a diver or a swivel and spoon makes a single change.

The third reason is your ability to drop and vertically jig the lure if you happen to notice something enticing on the fishfinder, such as an unexpected hole or drop-off. In windy or high-current conditions you may need a little more weight, but generally speaking a half an ounce will allow you to at least probe the water down to 15' or 20' when you unexpectedly see something you like. Again, this is a tremendous advantage.

Flexibility is the key. Using the leadhead/jig combination provides you with options, options, and more options, which means you can provide the fish with options, options, and more options. With a Fin-S or a twister tail, for example, the jig will run relatively deep so long as you give it time to sink after the initial cast. Swap it out for a shad-body, however, and it will sink slower and run shallower. Change over to a paddle-tail and it will spin on the fall, which occasionally triggers the bites more than any other form of drop or retrieve. You find some fish that are eating off the bottom, when you give the lure a slow hop? Put on a tube jig body with floating plastic filaments, and catch 'em up. The flexibility these options provides for you in your quest to find the most effective color, depth, or pattern at any given time is, in my opinion, so valuable it justifies starting off each and every shallow water casting trip with a jig head on the end of the line.

What about color? As with the spoon, generally speaking, you'll want to match the color of your lure to the color of the water. Here's another list for you that generally holds true but once again, remember, this information is rule of thumb—not cold, hard fact. Also remember to put those options to good use; when you're not catching fish, change colors, patterns, and tail styles often.

• In relatively clear and/or milky water, white, silver, or light smoke colors are often the winner.

• In muddy water, reds, browns, and purples usually do the trick.

• In tannic-stained brownish water, gold and rootbeer are top choices. Often, rootbeer with gold flecks of glitter molded into the plastic out-produce the regular variety. This is also excellent water for using gold spoons and/or spinnerbaits.

• In greenish water, chartreuse or lime green usually take top honors. Yellow and drab gray can also be quite effective in greenish water.

• In the dark or extremely low-light conditions, black, dark purple, and dark greens often out-produce other choices.

• Bubblegum and pink have varied effectiveness, which is (so far as I can tell) extremely unpredictable. You'll see days where the fish slaughter it in clear water, and others when they love pink in off-colored water. The next week pink could be a complete bust. This is a color you should definitely keep in the box and give it a shot whenever the catch is not up to expectations; you never know when it'll prove to be the hot ticket.

• In all different conditions, the all-around best color is (in my opinion—ten excellent anglers will give you ten other "best" all-around colors) a half-and-half pumpkinseed/chartreuse combination. This color pattern will work in virtually all water conditions and two out of three times, works better than anything else.

What about all those fancy patterns with bars and stripes and wavy designs? Those are meant to catch your eye in the tackle shop more than they are to catch the fish's eye in the water. There are a few exceptions but generally speaking solids or half-and-half color patterns are more effective on any given day than those fancy patterns.

Should you choose a paddle tail, a twister, or a shad body? Again, the effectiveness of each will vary depending on the conditions. Generally speaking, when the fish are feeding on menhaden, shad bodies may draw their interest a little quicker. If they're eating bay anchovies, a Fin-S or twister tail style is likely to hold more attraction. When it comes to stripers, in my experience twister tails hold the top position by a slim margin over shad bodies, Fin-S, paddle tails, and tube jigs, in that order.

So—you've taken the type of lure, color pattern, and body shape into account. There's yet another variable we need to consider: size. In virtually every condition, this is a match-the-hatch scenario. If the stripers are feeding on tiny anchovies, pick out a three-inch tail with a slender profile. If they're on peanut bunker, bull minnow, and silversides, go to four inches. When larger stripers are eating perch and the like, push it up to a six-inch bait. And if you're shallow water casting for trophy-sized fish, go to eight inch tails. Obviously, you'll have to increase the size of your jig head to more or less match the size of the overall bait. So—where do you start? A four-inch tail is the most versatile in most conditions.

Wait a sec—on second thought size isn't the last factor. There's also scent to consider. What about those flavored or scented plastics, and salt-impregnated lures? Do these really make a difference? When you're getting a reaction bite from a fast retrieve, their effect is minimal if it exists at all. But when you're fishing the bait slowly or hopping it over the bottom, there's no doubt in my mind that scent-impregnated baits like Berkley Gulps or Powerbaits and Mister Twister Exudes absolutely positively are more effective than completely unscented baits. (I've been unable to convince myself that salt-impregnation makes any difference whatsoever.) Why am I so sure? Three reasons: first off, I've seen too many occasions where fish have picked up and eaten scented plastic jigs that were sitting on bottom. They don't tend to do that with regular plastics. Secondly, I've seen too many occasions where fish grabbed scented jigs and through some angler error, were allowed to run with the jig and the hook was not set. These fish usually swallowed the jig entirely.

Thirdly, personal experience has convinced me that I catch more fish when using them.

Some of today's plastics are so incredibly stinky they even out-odor the real deal. Berkley's Gulp! is the prime example. The manufacturer claims it has 400-times the scent dispersion of other baits, and this isn't just some wild guess. John Prochnow, one of the in-house scientists at Pure Fishing, described to me how they actually arrived at this number: by running tests on the Gulp!s with an instrument called a spectrometer. This measured the actual amount of molecules being disbursed in the water, and on a scientific basis, is pretty darn hard to argue with. And Berkley didn't stop there. Before introducing Gulp!s to the market, they tested them on a number of different species. These fish were kept in a pool with a mechanical "boat" that towed the lures. In order to be sure the fish weren't thrown off their feed by the surroundings, the scientists ran the boat around the pool continually for days before introducing baits behind it. Then they recorded how the fish reacted to the baits, measured how long they would hold them after grabbing one, and so on.

So—do these lures work 400-times as well as other lures when it comes to catching fish? Not a chance. But they do work darn good, and in the hands of an angler who's used to them, may well out-fish the real thing. In the dark I've found them extremely effective and you'll do best by rigging them with a straight hook or on a very light head, and retrieving them slowly to allow the scent trail to build as it moves through the water. Also, replace them after 45 minutes or so, past which time Gulp!s lose some of their effectiveness.

One other very interesting tidbit that comes from Prochnow: Berkley also tested different substances to see what repelled fish, as well as testing to see what attracted them. Surprisingly, one thing that everyone thinks of as a fish repellent turned out to have zero effect on the fish—gasoline. Evidently the scent and taste receptors in a fish are shaped such that they don't even register gas. As Prochnow put it, "It's like trying to fit a square peg into a round hole; the molecules simply don't fit." But DEET, the active ingredient in the vast majority of bug repellents, turned out to be a huge turn-off to fish. And of course, bugs can be a killer when shallow water fishing, and using bug juice is often a must. Try to avoid using it in the first place, but when you feel like you must apply bug repellent, be sure to wash your hands with soap and water afterwards.

So there you have it: the go-to lure. All things being equal, on an average day with average conditions, virtually every time I take my first throw when light tackle casting for stripers there's a scent-impregnated four-inch chartreuse/pumpkinseed Powerbait twister tail (or Vibro-worm tail) rigged with a half-ounce jig head on the end of the line. The three-inch Gulp! chartreuse Inshore twister tail would be the next lure in line. Don't allow yourself to get stuck on any one bait, though. If I'm in a spot where I believe feeding fish are and I take the first five or six casts without getting a strike, that tail gets ripped right off and a "best guess" is made as to what color and pattern will be more effective depending on the conditions of the moment.

Tactics

Okay, you have the perfect gear in your hands and the ideal lure on the end of your line. The spot is a good one, the tide is right, and the sun hasn't broken the horizon yet. You cast and cast, yet catch no fish. What's the deal? The way you retrieve can be every bit as important as what you retrieve. This is yet another variable that must be felt-out. There's no way to predict what type of retrieve will excite the fish at any given moment, short of figuring out the pattern and matching it. There are, however, two more generalizations we can make on this count. First off, the cooler the water is the slower the fish usually want the retrieve to be, and the warmer it is, the faster they'll want it. Secondly, early and late in the day when the sun is low on the horizon they tend to strike higher in the water column, and the brighter the sun, the lower in the water column they'll usually strike. Beyond that, the fish's preference at any given moment is likely to change with the tide, wind-driven currents, amount of boat traffic, and forage type.

When you first arrive at a spot, begin retrieving bearing these factors in mind. If it's early in the morning on a chilly October day, for example, start off with a relatively slow retrieve high in the water column. If it's full light in June, start off with a relatively fast retrieve low in the water column; up- or down-size your leadhead if necessary, to get the jig running at the proper speed in the proper depth zone.

If you don't get any strikes right off the bat when you're fishing the jig up top, try letting the jig sink for a three-count. Still no hits? Let it drop for five, then seven, and so on until it's resting on bottom when you begin the retrieve. Also vary the style; try a few casts with a steady retrieval rate, then try a few with an erratic speed. You've yet to have a bite after trying all these different retrieval combinations? It's time to move, or try a different color or lure. As mentioned earlier, you should maintain your flexibility and be quick to pull up stakes and try a new spot. The number-one problem most shallow water anglers have is that they're slow to move on from a spot they know (or think they know) holds fish. Many guys will pull up to a good shallow water point, drop an anchor, and spend the next half-hour there. Cast after cast after cast produces no results, yet still they remain. Meanwhile, they could be putting that time to good use, prospecting or hitting other hotspots. My personal rule of thumb? If I don't catch fish in the first five minutes, I'm usually out of there. 10 minutes, at an absolute max. And if I catch one or two then take 10 casts without a hit, it's time to move on. Now—let's say you've followed all these suggestions and everything should be perfect, yet you still catch no fish. Sounds like it's time to change tactics altogether, and try fishing deeper water in some other fashion.

CHAPTER FIVE

JIGGING FOR ROCKFISH
Often producing a mixed-bag, jigging allows the use of light gear for big fish.

Jigging is another tactic many anglers enjoy because it's another light-tackle game. Essentially, jigging is lowering a lure to the approximate depth of the fish, then raising and lowering your rod tip to impart a life-like action to your lure. It's most effective when fish are schooled up and also works quite well for catching larger than average fish when the average fish are on top, busting water. Since you'll be more or less vertically positioned over the fish, it's important for the captain to be able to locate them and either position and

Note the light rod-big fish combo—jigging is a fun way to hook into big fish with light gear!

hold the boat over the school, or position the boat for a drift over the school.

There are no hard and fast rules as to the where's and when's of jigging. You can try this tactic any time fish are schooled up, either in open water or along an edge, break, or other form of underwater structure. It does require a decent fishfinder and an operator who knows how to read it, although there are some old-timers out there who can position a boat over some form of structure they're intimately familiar with by simply looking at distant landmarks.

Since the fish need to be schooled to effectively jig them up, this tactic is not usually applied early in the season. Migrating fish will be nearly impossible to catch by jigging, and the technique usually becomes better and better as the season progresses and fish pack tighter and tighter together. Once fish start breaking water, jigging becomes much easier. Throughout the fall months birds often mark the spot for you, and boat position becomes a matter of parking where you see them. Why not just cast to the breaking fish? That would certainly get you a bent rod. But the larger stripers usually patrol just below the school of breaking fish, waiting for an easy meal to drift down to them. Since you can drop below the smaller guys and jig your lure at the depth the larger fish are hanging at, you have a much better chance of catching lunkers from a school of stripers busting water if you drop a jig down instead of casting.

One important note: You don't want to drive those fish down from the surface, because they make it easy to spot the school with your eyes. So never drive directly into the fish. Instead, approach them from up-wind (or up-current, whichever is strongest,) and once you're within 50 or 60 yards cut back to idle speed. Once you're within 30' or 40' of the fish shut down the motor, and allow the wind to push your dead boat over them.

How does one know when to jig? As mentioned earlier, often jigging is a great way to fish when other bites flatten out. You can also count on it working effectively when small fish are feeding on the surface; quite often, as long as the water is 30' or deeper, there will be a few big stripers holding down deep below even when the fish up top are a mere 12". Any time you spot suspended, schooled fish, you can try jigging them. It's often a good game plan to try jigging briefly when you arrive at a spot where you had intended to chum or bottom fish, too. This gives you a shot at getting some quick fish into the boat without having to deal with dropping the anchor, prepping chum, or any other of the actions that are necessary but cut into actual fishing time.

Jigging is probably the most effective method you can possibly use when fish are in medium to small size schools which are moving around a lot. You may find this situation on a long, uninterrupted channel edge, or in open water when there are fast-moving pockets of bait scattered around. Often this occurs shortly after the spawn, in late spring and/or early summer. In these situations jigging is the best way to get a lure presented to the fish the moment you locate them on the fishfinder, without getting bogged down with bait, anchors, setting spreads, and the like. As soon as the fish move on you can, too, without any break-down time. In these situations don't just drift around and jig—you've got to hunt those fish. Keep on the move and keep a close eye on the meter at all times. When you see the fish be ready (and have all your anglers be ready) to drop immediately, and jig for all they're worth until the boat drifts off the fish or they leave. As soon as the fish disappear, keep the lines up until you relocate them. Yes, you'll spend a lot of time searching if you fish this way. But at the end of the day, you'll have more stripers in the cooler than the guy who drifted around and jigged the whole time, hoping to luck into the fish.

One other time jigging is the best way to go: extremely early in the spring, when the first of the big spawners begin their approach to the freshwater areas, pods of them are sometimes marked by gannets flying overhead. This is common in the Chesapeake and also up north in New Jersey and New York waters, inside Lower Bay and the Sandy Hook area, then later towards the mouth of the Hudson. Usually these fish can be targeted during the month of March, by putting around with a good pair of binoculars and keeping a sharp eye out for those gannets. Remember that these won't be huge flocks of diving birds like you'll see in the fall. Expect to find patches of three to seven gannets at a time, and rarely more than 10. They'll usually be on the move, but will circle and make occasional dives at times. This is when you'll want to pull up and drop large jigs or jigging spoons. Even though birds mark the spot, the stripers will usually be well below the surface. Have one angler on the boat keep his offering near bottom, another at mid depth, and so on to cover the water column from the bottom up to about 20' below the boat, until you spot the fish on the fishfinder and can more accurately pinpoint their depth.

Tackle

When it comes to jigging, you'll need a lot more versatility in your tackle choice. Rod and reel size, as well as line test, will have to be matched to the size of the lures you jig, which will in turn be matched to the depth of the water you're fishing in and at times, the speed of the current. In any case, you'll want a rod with a fairly slow action, so you can keep a bend in the tip at all times whether you're on the up-swing or the down-swing. Nine times out of ten your lure will be hit as it falls. If you have a fast action rod with little bend in the tip, it'll be much tougher to keep constant tension on the line as your lure falls and accordingly, will be tougher to recognize when a fish has hit the lure. A six to seven foot rod works fine for this purpose, and in most situations, a medium weight rig which can handle 12 to 17 pound test will do the job. Braid is the line of choice for this type of fishing. You'll feel far more hits and sink far more hooks solidly with braid, thanks to the absence of stretch.

So far as reels go, this is one type of fishing where spinning reels out-class conventional gear. There are two reasons why: the first is that you'll be constantly letting out or reeling in line to keep your jig at the appropriate depth. With conventional gear this forces you to constantly take your right hand off the crank handle to put the reel into freespool. You can guess what happens next—that is practically guaranteed to be the exact moment when the fish strikes. Secondly, once you get into a jigging rhythm your body will want to keep it up. One half of your brain will tell your right hand to release the reel into freespool to drop some line, but the other half of your brain will continue telling your other hand to jerk the rod up. The net result is instant backlash. This happens to the best of us after a few hours of doing the yo-yo routine, but it won't be a problem with spinning gear. While you jig with a spinner, you can shift your left hand to the bail to release it and drop line on the up-swing without fears of backlash. As you move your hand back to the crank flip the bailer back shut. At all times you'll be ready to react to the strike, without creating a tangled mess. One must, however, be careful to choose a spinning reel with infinite anti-reverse. If there's any kick-back on the up-swing with a heavy metal jig on the end of the line, you'll trash your reel in short order.

Another piece of tackle which is imperative when jigging is a good swivel. Reach into your tacklebox right now, pick out all the 25-cent brass barrel swivels, and toss them into the trash can. It never ceases to amaze me how people will spend tens of thousands of dollars on their boat, hundreds of dollars on fuel, hundreds more on assorted tackle and gear, then buy the 25-cent swivels. Do you ever have line-twist problems? If so, there's a 99-percent chance that this is why. This goes for other forms of fishing as well as jigging, but it's really important when you know your lure will be fluttering and spinning constantly throughout the day. And those cheap barrel swivels simply don't turn. You need a ball-bearing swivel. Not just any ball-bearing swivel, either. Look in a well-stocked store, and you'll note some ball bearing swivels attach directly to the clip, and others have an extra ring between the clip and the ball bearing. Those with no extra ring sometimes slide up against the clip, and bind themselves in place. That extra ring, however, prevents this problem and keeps the ball-bearing turning. Now look at the ring your line ties to. Some swivels have a split ring here, but more expensive ones have a welded ring. What's the difference? If you ever hook a 30 pound fish, you'll discover it has the muscle to bend that split ring open. Bye-bye, fish—buy the swivels with welded rings.

The lure itself used for jigging can vary from spoons to lead-heads to bucktails. The one thing all lures used for jigging must have in common? They need some weight. In water under 20' with light winds and currents, a one-ounce jig is all you need to keep in contact with the bottom, with this size gear. But in 50' depths with a roaring current, four or five ounces will become necessary. The weight of the lure is not the only thing coming into play here, however. Shape also has a big effect. Hammered metal spoons like a Hopkins tend to sink faster than leadhead jigs with plastic bodies, even when the jig's weight equals that of the spoon. Maria jigs are an excellent example—these "spoons" are long, thin plastic epoxy hardened over colored reflective tape. For their size, they weigh significantly less than metal jigging spoons. Yet because of their hydrodynamic shape, they sink every bit as fast as metal spoons that are twice the weight. Plus, these jigs catch fish, and that makes them an excellent choice

A selection of jigging spoons. Focus on chartreuse, blue/green, red/white, pink and plain silver color patterns.

for light tackle users.

Some other spoons you'll want to consider using include the Braid, Hopkins, and Yo-Zuri metal jigging spoons. All of these sink well and will catch fish. Hopkins are limited to silver with or without feathers, while the Braids and Yo-Zuris come in a gazillion different color patterns. Generally speaking, greens, blues and pinks should command top billing. Shimano Butterfly jigs are big in the news lately, but due to supply shortages are not readily available in most areas. I haven't been able to get hold of them yet as of the time of this writing, so I'm taking a wait-and-see attitude. Stingsilvers are an old favorite for jiggers. They have wider bodies than most of the others mentioned here and tend to flutter down slower than most comparable spoons, so plan to use them only when you are not concerned about getting deep with minimal weight. You will also find, in some tackle shops, custom-made "bomb" jigs which are really no more than in-line torpedo weights which are painted and have a hook attached to one eye. These are quite effective at times, particularly when jigging extra-deep and you need maximum mass. Try the ones that are one half red and one half yellow. You can also make them yourself by heating a lead weight with a blow torch then dipping it into powder paint.

In water shallower than 25' or in areas of little to no current on windless days, that same leadhead jig with a plastic body you use for shallow water casting is a good choice for jigging. You'll probably want to go to at least a one-ounce head, but by jigging with this lure you get all of the same advantages as when casting: quick color and pattern changes, plus the added bonus of multiple strikes. With metal jigs, one strike is usually all you'll get from a single fish, as they quickly realize the "fish" fluttering around in front of them doesn't taste very good. With the plastics, however, they will often strike the same lure over and over again until they find the hook.

Added Bonus	**Added Deficit**
If there are flounder in the area you'll pick up a lot more of them jigging with plastics than you will with metal jigging spoons.	*If there are bluefish in the area they'll shred your plastics quickly, while spoons usually go unharmed.*

Bucktails can also be jigged, and they are a good choice when the fish are lethargic on jigs and you need to tease them with bait. Normally, the fish you hook while jigging will be hitting the jig because of a sight-activated reaction strike. Interestingly, it's a different feeding mode than the fish you take while utilizing other modes of fishing, such as chumming. Take schoolie stripers in the middle Chesapeake region during the month of September, for example. Let's say you chum through the peak of the tide at The Hill, with good action. Then, as slack water hits, the bite drops off. Pull the anchor, tie on jigs, and shuffle over to the 30' to 60' drop on the eastern edge (the Hill Hole). Locate a mass of fish on the fishfinder in this area, and you can often get these fish to strike jigs without a problem. But there's a reverse effect, too. When that chumming bite is running strong, you may find that jigging produces few fish. Scent and/or taste—sometimes one that's identical to the scent/taste being introduced into the water via the chum—is necessary to generate the strike. What does this have to do with bucktails? They allow you to cross over between artificials and baits, to some degree. You can tip them with live bull minnow, peeler crab chunks, cut fish, or squid, and tease both the scent/taste and sight-generated reactions.

Feather jigs (which look like bucktails but are tied with chicken feathers, instead of deer tail hair or nylon) are another tool that should be in every jiggers arsenal. When rigged properly, they can be cast and jigged as opposed to dropped and vertically jigged. This

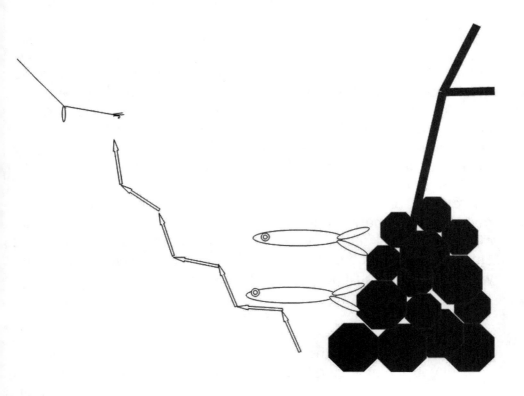

Feather jigging is an ideal way to reach fish you can't position the boat over, such as those hugging lighthouse rockpiles, or un-approachable bridge pilings.

allows you to use them in situations where you can't position the boat directly over the fish, either because of close proximity to rocks or pilings, strong currents or winds, or spooky fish. Note the specific rig, as shown in the illustration. (Note: good feather jigs can be hard to come by. Fishbone's Bait & Tackle, in Pasadena, MD, 410-360-0573, is a good, reliable source for top-notch jigs.) It consists of a triple swivel with a clip attached to a bank sinker, a three to four foot leader of supple 20 to 30 pound test monofilament, and a "popeye" style feather jig trimmed with chicken feathers. Fish this rig by casting it out in the direction of the fish, and allowing it to sink until it hits bottom. Then reel until the line is taunt, with the rod pointed directly at the jig. Begin to jig by raising the rod tip quickly and firmly to the 11 o'clock position. Then allow the rod tip to drop back towards the jig while reeling in all slack at the same time. As soon as the rod is pointed down at the jig again, sweep it up with another jigging motion. Continue jigging and reeling in this fashion, without breaking the rhythm, until the weight breaks the surface. It's very important to follow this retrieval/jigging method to a tee. Don't stop in the middle of the retrieve, and don't only allow it to sink half way. Establishing the rhythm is extremely important, and what you'll discover is that quite often stripers will follow the feather jig up from the depths but won't strike until it nears the surface. Break the rhythm when it's still halfway down, and you'll never know the fish was interested.

Tactics

When you have the right lure on the end of the line, how successful you are at jigging becomes a matter of two techniques: boat positioning and rod motion. Boat positioning is probably more important than rod motion, but only because you can't jig 'em up if they don't see your jigs. But you can have two or three people standing side by side, jigging at the same time with the same gear, and one will catch twice as many fish as the others. The motion they impart to their jig and the timing of their hook-sets makes all the difference in the world.

First, the jigging motion: in its purest form, jigging is simply moving the rod up and down to jerk the lure up and down. How fast should you go? Usually, raising that rod tip as fast as you can without peeling line from a properly set drag, is your best bet. Jigging is an active technique used to stimulate a reaction strike, and jigging upward slowly gives the fish more time to eyeball the offering, which is bad, because you don't want them to observe the lure. Instead, you want them to catch a glimpse of it flashing as it darts upwards, perking their interest. Then, you want to generate a gut reaction to strike from the fish when it sees the lure fluttering back down.

If you've ever watched an injured fish in its last throes, you'll understand why the dart up/flutter down motion is so effective. Fish that can no longer control themselves well enough to swim tend to put a burst of energy into an attempt to swim towards the surface. When the energy runs out, they sink and flutter towards the bottom. If they gather enough steam they will repeat the motion, time and time again.

Nine times out of 10, fish will hit the lure (or an injured, struggling baitfish, for that matter,) as it falls through the water. A good angler will detect the strike most of the time, but if there is any slack in the line you're apt to miss it sometimes. This is another good argument for lifting the tip vigorously; quite often this will end up being your hook-setting motion by default, because you never detected the take. When the strike does go undetected, gentle lifts will turn into inadvertent and ineffective hook sets.

Some anglers swear that a jerky, erratic motion is better for the up-swing. In most cases, however, experience will prove that you will catch more fish if you stick with a smooth sweep up, and a smooth drop down. Speaking of the up-sweep: you'll want to raise that rod tip high, so that when you lower it again the jig has several feet to fall and fish that are four or five feet above or below your target zone will get a glimpse of it. Be careful, however, not to overextend your arm and raise the tip as high as possible over your head. If you do so and a fish hits the jig during the first foot or so of the fall, you won't have the ability to bring the rod up enough to set the hook effectively. Instead, keep your elbow cocked next to your body and stop the up-swing at 10 o'clock or so.

Of course, you just knew there had to be an exception. And there are two. Whenever you're jigging a bucktail that's tipped with a live or fresh bait, you may want to be a little gentler on the up-swing. Otherwise, the bait is likely to be jerked off or shredded when a fish nips at it, while you jig the rod. And you will encounter situations—usually when the fish are holding extremely close to bottom or a chunk of structure—in which a quick snap of the wrist raising the tip a mere foot or two is more effective than jigging with long sweeps.

Just how are you going to detect strikes, with all that up and down motion? A big part of the equation is learning how to allow the lure to sink unrestricted so it can flutter and sway in an attractive manner, yet still maintain constant tension on the line so you feel it when a striper pops the lure. Remember that in the Tackle section of this chapter, it specified using a rod with a slow-action tip—this is why. With a tip that will bend six or eight inches, you have a little bit of room to play as you drop down, allowing the lure to fall unencumbered yet still maintaining tension on the line and rod. Bottom line: if you're slowing the lure's rate of sink you're reducing its effectiveness, but if you allow your line to go slack as it sinks you've more or less eliminated your ability to detect strikes. You need to find that happy medium. One exception: when fishing with light lures, it is sometimes possible to watch your slack line as it sinks, where it meets the water. Hits can be detected visually, when you see a sudden jerk in the line.

Of course, even if you maintain tension perfectly, there will be times that you don't feel the strike. On these occasions, you may simply note that your lure stops falling before it should. When your lure is being jigged close to bottom so that it touches on the very end of the fall, but it suddenly stops half way through the fall, take the hint—a fish has grabbed it and it's time for an immediate hook-set.

What depth should you be jigging at? Not always right on bottom, though this will be the best zone much of the time. Judge by your fishfinder. When you see fish suspended at mid-depth give it a shot, and when you see them sitting at or near bottom try dropping there. That said, when you see a big school of fish running through a large range on the fishfinder, try jigging as low as possible in the school or just above bottom. Generally speaking, you'll find the largest fish in the school shadowing the mass of fish, slightly below and often behind the main group. If you are jigging on bottom you don't want your lure to hit until your rod tip is at or near the very lowest point of the sweep. This way, you'll still be able to utilize the full upsweep. If you start getting hit when your lure just begins to fall after a broad sweep up off the bottom, take the hint—the fish are feeding higher in the water column. Crank in four or five feet of line and you'll keep the lure in the strike zone for more time.

Added Jigging Bonus

When jigging at or near the bottom, you have a shot at picking up flounder and sea trout as well as stripers, if they're in the area. Try dead-sticking for a few seconds for trout, and keep the jig active but allow it to bounce off bottom for flounder.

CHAPTER SIX

TROLLING

When what you're after is meat.

Trolling can be easily summed up thusly: you putt along at slow speeds dragging a multitude of lures behind the boat. The motion of the boat combined with the shape or design of the lure imparts the swimming action, and the angler is out of the picture until the fish has struck and is solidly hooked on the line. There are many advantages to this technique: one knowledgeable angler can set up the lines and operate the boat, allowing a boatload of inexperienced anglers to reel in fish after fish; the constant motion of the boat isn't

Trolling is an extremely productive method of fishing, and in many cases, this is the best way to load your cooler. The rig seen here is a Billy Bar.

tiring and doesn't require the angler to "work," as when casting or jigging; it is extremely effective in many circumstances; it allows you to keep your lures in a specific depth zone; it allows you to cover multiple depth zones with different lures at the same time; and it eliminates messy bait, chum, and the like. There are, however, a few disadvantages as well: because of the large weights and significant pressure on the line at all times heavy gear is a necessity in most trolling situations; when multi-line trolling tangles occur they can be absolutely disastrous; when large numbers of boats are trolling in the same area it can get chaotic; and for some people, listening to the engine drone on all day can become tiring. Despite the down-sides, it must be stressed again: there are some situations in which trolling is the most effective way to catch stripers, in extreme cases by a margin of 10 to one or even larger.

There are many different forms of trolling: light tackle trolling, heavy tackle trolling, wire-lining, and bottom-bouncing. Since each of these are fairly different forms of fishing, we'll approach each on a one-by-one basis in each section the specific method applies to. Note that these are just the basic techniques. The number of trolling techniques practiced by anglers up and down the coast is literally infinite, with different tweaks and changes made to tackle and tactics to target specific fish in specific situations. Understand these four basic methods, however, and you'll have the building blocks to troll effectively for stripers in just about any place or season.

Choosing when to troll is often a matter of necessity. When migrating fish are scattered out as they go to and from their spawning areas, for example, you'll usually have to troll and cover a ton of water if you want to catch large numbers of these fish. Many anglers call it "collision fishing" because you need to simply drive around until a fish happens to intersect with one of your lures. Trolling may also be necessary when the fish are holding relatively deep in a fast-current area, where jigging or bait fishing is nearly impossible. In these cases, wire-lining is the prescription for catching fish. And when fish are scattered over a large area in a tributary river mouth or basin, again, covering ground may be the key to catching fish and light tackle trolling comes into its own.

Tackle (Light)

When it comes to light tackle trolling, all the doors are open. Spinning gear, conventional, whatever you prefer up to the 20 pound class should be able to do the job. Commonly, light tackle trollers will use the same rods and reels they use for jigging or chumming. Rod action, length, and weight aren't as important to match to the technique because the rod and line will be under constant pressure as the boat travels along. Either monofilament or braid lines will work fine, but once again, use only top-notch swivels—if a lure starts spinning on the troll or if you're pulling spoons which spin constantly, using a cheap swivel is a guaranteed recipe for disaster. Leaders aren't usually necessary when trolling such light gear, although you may want to add a few feet of heavier leader if large fish or bluefish are in the area.

Lures commonly used for light tackle trolling cover a wide spectrum: small spoons, lipped diving plugs, and twister tail or shad body jigs, will all be effective. Rat-L-Traps and similar swimming plugs are particularly effective when light tackle trolling for stripers, especially when peanut bunker are in the area (usually from mid-summer through the fall). Since your gear is light you won't want to add weight to these lures. So, plan to use divers like the Rat-L-Trap or lipped Rapalas when the fish are hitting five or 10' below the surface, and troll spoons or jigs when the fish are feeding right up top. This is a great way to take fish from a school of breaking stripers which acts skittish if you attempt to drive up close and cast. Merely troll around the periphery of the school, with lures like these deployed.

Tackle (Heavy)

For both heavy tackle trolling and specialized forms of trolling like wire-lining you'll want to run 40 to 50 pound test on conventional reels like the old stand-by Penn Senators or level winder reels. Line counter reels are also good since they allow you to get very specific with your line lengths when you deploy your trolling gear. Wire line (monel or stainless) and braid both cut the water better than monofilament and as a result they will run deeper with the same amount of weight than mono will. When you need to get deep in strong current areas, these are the lines you'll want to be working with.

Leaders vary depending on the lure in play. Many, such as umbrellas or Stretch 25's, don't require any leader at all. For others, such as tandem rigs, leaders are extremely important. Generally speaking, 50 to 60 pound test is plenty for a leader, though when heavy lures and trophy size fish come into play, many captains will opt up to 80 pound test. When choosing leaders remember that fluorocarbon has the lowest visibility, but in all but the clearest waters it's tough to "prove" it works any better than quality mono. It is very stiff, however, and thus has excellent abrasion resistance. Softer lines will abrade slightly more easily, but they also allow the lure on the end of the line to move with a hair more freedom. Plus, they have more stretch which can absorb some of the errors often made when leadering a large fish to the boat by hand. That said, I always use fluorocarbons. You pick your own poison.

Rod action is really a matter of preference more than anything else. Roller guides are unnecessary unless you're running wire, which will last longer if you have roller tips on the end of the rod. And many good anglers feel a slow action tip works a little better when trolling with wire or braid, since it has some give when the fish hits. Otherwise, if there's no give in the rod or line, the hook may rip out of the fish a little more often.

Lures used for trolling range widely, depending on both geography and seasonality. The chart shown here covers the basics. Note that you might see any applied in any particular area at any given time, and this merely shows their traditional uses.

When it comes to trolling, bottom-bouncing is in a class of its own. It's the only form of trolling that requires an angler to constantly work the rod, and it is usually used to target specific fish in a specific spot. Like heavy tackle trolling and wire lining it requires some pretty stout gear, with reels of the same type. Monel wire line is usually used for this tactic, and rods should be fiberglass (read: more or less unbreakable) with a slow action tip. Unlike other forms of trolling you'll actually be able to detect the strike when wire-lining, and you must be able to feel the weight hitting bottom for the tactic to work; the slow action rod will make this easier.

NC/VA/MD Coastal	MD Chesapeake	DE/NJ/NY Coastal and Northern Areas
--Umbrella rigs dressed w/plastic shad bodies	--Umbrella rigs dressed w/plastic shad bodies	--Umbrella rigs dressed w/ spoons, flashers, and dodgers
--Large spoons incl. Tony Acetta 19/21, Huntington Drone, and Crippled Alwives	--Tandam rigs tied w/ bucktails and parachutes	--Umbrella rigs dressed w/surgical hoses
--Swimming plugs such as Mann's Stretch 25	--Spoons incl. Tony Acetta, Crippled Alwives, and Cathers	--Large bunker spoons & "Secret" spoons (spoons with heavy weights built in)
--Surgical hoses	--Billy Bars	--Spoons such as Tony Acettas and Crippled Alwives
--Mojo's	--Bucktails dressed w/ twister tails or pork rind	--Bucktails and parachutes dressed w/ twister tails, pork rind, or plastic shad bodies
--Daisy Chains	--Tandam rigs tied w/ large shad body plastics	--Surgical Hoses (sometimes called "tubes" or "snakes" up north)
	--Swimming plugs such as Mann's Stretch 25 and Stretch 15	--Swimming plugs such as Mann's Stretch 25
	--Surgical Hoses	
	--Daisy Chains	

You'll find that trolling lure choices vary greatly, depending on the region you're in. Truth be told, most of these lures will work most of the time in most of the region, and geographical tradition dictates their choice more than effectiveness.

Lures used for bottom-bouncing are very specific: bucktails in the three to six inch range, usually white, chartreuse, or yellow. They should have light heads, usually an ounce or a fraction of an ounce. And they are usually tipped with big, live bull minnow, twister tails, squid strips, or (for traditionalists) pork rinds.

Bottom bouncing rigs start off with a triple swivel, tied to the end of the main line. One of the two remaining eyes of the swivel needs a three-foot dropper line, which should be relatively light mono; 20 pound test works well. (If you use heavier line for the dropper and if the weight snags bottom, you'll lose the entire rig. But the 20 pound test will break off before your main line does, saving your lures and swivels.) Tie a six to 10 ounce dipsy or bank sinker to the end of the

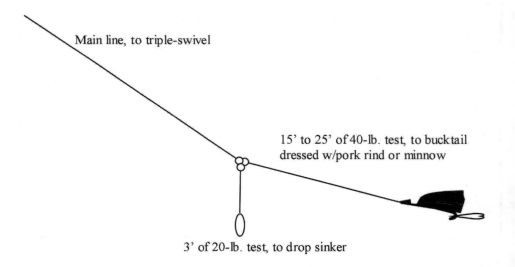

Main line, to triple-swivel

15' to 25' of 40-lb. test, to bucktail dressed w/pork rind or minnow

3' of 20-lb. test, to drop sinker

The bottom-bouncing rig. Traditionally, the bucktail is dressed with a pork rind or live bull minnow, but twister tails also work well.

dropper line; the exact size depends on the depth you're fishing. In 20' to 25' six will usually do the trick; in 25' to 30' you'll need to go to eight ounces, and deeper means even more lead is necessary. The third eye of the dropper is for your leader, which is commonly 40 or 50 pound test. In this case it should be a long one, no less than 15'. Many old-timers use 20' or even 25' leaders. To the end of the leader, tie on that dressed bucktail.

Tactics (Light)

There are several situations when light tackle trolling should be your tactic of choice, but they all hinge on one basic factor: the fish must be feeding (or at least willing to feed) on three to six inch baitfish at or near the surface. Trolling in a tributary with light tackle early in the spring, when most of the bait in the tributaries is likely to be adults making their spawning run, is not likely to lead to much success. In that same tributary during the early fall, however, when small baitfish are migrating out towards bigger water—and stripers are waiting to intercept them—can lead to banner catches.

Another situation in which light tackle trolling is a good bet occurs when schoolie stripers are scattered along a channel edge or drop-off which has a plateau with water 15' or shallower at the top, and 20' or deeper at the bottom. Keep your baits running along the edge but up on the plateau, and the stripers will strike them. Light tackle can also be trolled effectively along banks and edges with sharp, sudden drop-offs. Sod banks in Jersey's coastal bays provide the perfect example; while most anglers will cast and retrieve lures here, if you find a long, relatively straight bank with a near-vertical drop-off, trolling light tackle close to the shore line is often very productive. Note that if the fish are spooky, you can take a lesson from the reservoir guys. Guides working in some striper lakes such as Lake Anna, in Virginia, learned early on that reservoir stripers can be quite spooky at times. So can the saltwater variety, of course, but with the fish in freshwater it seemed even more so. To make light tackle trolling even more effective, these guides started trolling with side planers. These are simply smaller versions of the big planer boards used by virtually every charter captain on the Chesapeake, and they are available in most major tackle shops. The side planers will take your line out and away from your boat, allowing you to troll 50' or 60' away from a bank or drop-off while your lure is a mere five or six feet off the bank or drop-off. Not only does this tactic come in handy when the fish are skittish, it also works well when you're trolling in an area with a highly variable bottom close to shore, and must worry about running aground. Note, however, that most of the store-bought side planers are small compared to bay-worthy planer boards, and in rough water won't do the trick.

The most popular and often practiced application for light tackle trolling, however, is when fish are breaking water. Every practiced striper angler has been through this before: you run up to diving birds and breaking fish, slow down, and putt to within casting distance. As soon as you're positioned well for casting, the fish dive and the birds break up. You may get in a successful cast or two before the fish sound, then the action dies right off. 15 minutes later the school pops up again, this time a quarter mile away. You repeat the process. Sound familiar? When the fish are a bit skittish and this what you go through, it's definitely time to try trolling light gear.

Instead of running up close to the fish, slow down when you're several hundred yards away. Deploy a few light tackle trolling lines, and head for the periphery of the school at a mere two MPH or so. You'll notice that you can troll around the edges of the school all day long, and as long as you don't drive right through it, they'll stay up for much longer than when you drove in and cast. Why? There may not be any solid evidence, but most seasoned anglers will agree that the fish are more disturbed by abrupt changes then they are by a constant sound. When you run for the school then come off of plane, you create a change in prop and exhaust noise—which the fish can certainly detect. Then you putt up close to the school and shift out of gear, causing another change the fish can detect. If you have a two-stroke outboard motor, remember that it'll make even more underwater noise idling in neutral than it will when in gear and running.

Yet if you slowly troll around the edges of the school, you're making a low-key, constant noise that really doesn't seem to bother the fish as much. So often, light tackle trolling will lead to significantly better catches than casting and retrieving will, when the fish are breaking water.

One more factor to remember when you choose whether or not to light tackle troll: consider the current. Strong flows will often make light tackle trolling tough. The little plugs, spoons, and jigs used with light gear can quickly become overpowered and turned on their side, or pushed right up to the surface. Think of this tactic as best applied when in slow-moving water.

Tactics (Heavy)

Trolling with heavy tackle is much more broad-based, and we'll have to break it down into several categories to take it all in: trolling for large, scattered, or migratory fish; trolling for schoolie stripers; trolling for ocean-run stripers; trolling for winter stripers, and trolling rips and high-current areas.

Trolling for large, scattered, or migratory fish is a top tactic for early spring striper fishing. On Chesapeake Bay during the trophy season, for example, you'll see 100 boats trolling for each you see chumming, jigging, or fishing with another method. Are those trollers catching more fish? Usually, though not always (more on this later in chapter 7). In fact, the vast majority of migrating fish taken up and down the coast during the spring months are caught by trolling. Migrators are a lot less interested in finding structure or a good feeding area and staging there than they are in completing their mission. So, you have to put a lure right in front of the fish's face to get it to eat. Trolling is one way to do that. Either by sheer luck or by the vast amount of water you cover, sooner or later, your trolling lures will collide with a fish. Remember that term, "collision fishing?"

The trolling spread we'll look at in a few pages (we need to cover some other ground, first!) is a rather extreme Chesapeake Bay charter trolling spread. Believe it or not, some captains will push this spread to include two dozen lines. Recreational anglers usually pull fewer than the 17 lines shown, to avoid the tangles that go along with towing a huge number of rods. In fact, few recreational anglers can handle more than eight or 10 lines, at most, and the majority of charter captains pull between eight and 12. How do those others get the spread so darn big? There are three keys to the charter boat's ability to run so many lines: their boats have huge beams, often as much as 12' while most recreational anglers are fishing from 8'6" wide boats; they have rodholders lining the gunwales, transom, and cabin top, while most recreational boats are limited to four in the gunwales and a set of rocket launchers on the top; and they use planer boards.

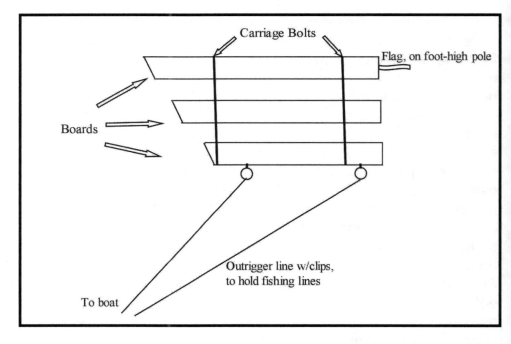

Most planer boards are assembled in garages and sheds. One of the few tackle shops to reliably carry them is Tochterman's, in Baltimore City (410/327-6942).

In both theory and application planer boards are no different than the side-planers used for years in freshwater fisheries, except that to be used on the bay they're built big. In fact, three foot planers are not out of line, and the size is necessary in heavy seas to prevent them from flipping over. Cannon does produce a set of plastic, two-board planer boards that will work (they go for about $100) but in heavy seas, you'll want heavy wood triple-boards. Most are built in sheds and garages, and I'm not aware of any commercially available models.

Making a set is fairly easy: cut your boards starting at three feet and going down in six-inch increments. Cut the leading edge of each board so it points out. Through-bolt them together, with three to four inches between each one. Screw in two eyes, one about a quarter of the way back and one at the rear. Run it out from the forward eye on a piece of clothes line, and run an outrigger line back through the rear eye. Note that each set of planer boards comes out a little different, and you'll probably have to adjust the forward eye fore or aft to find the best running position. You can use either heavy plastic clothes pins or outrigger release clips to hold your fishing lines. Most captains paint the board a bright color and add a flag to the outside board, to make it more visible and prevent cut-offs and tangles by other anglers. Naturally, you'll have to cut a mirror image of the planer board for the other side of the boat, just make sure the pattern is reversed—you need the boards to each run out in opposite directions from the boat.

The same basic spread as is shown here with planer boards in use, both with and without the boards and shaped to fit the local trends, is effective up and down the coast. It covers a huge swath of the water column, with the main emphasis on the upper 30' because that's where the trophies in the Chesapeake usually run at. To apply this spread to other areas in which the stripers may be running deeper than 30' you should swap out a couple of the lines for something more depth-appropriate; up in New York that would be considered a bunker spoon trolled with 10 or 12 ounces of lead on wire line, and down in North Carolina, it may take the form of a daisy chain run behind a 16 to 24 ounce cannonball weight. Interestingly, geography also plays a roll in what form umbrella rigs take. To the south, you'll find them made with plastic shad body teasers and a parachute/shad body hook bait. To the north, you're just as likely to find a series of small spoons rigged to each arm of the umbrella. Which works best? Neither and both—regardless of where you are on the coast. On any given day in any given place with any given conditions, one might out-fish the other... so you'd better bring both.

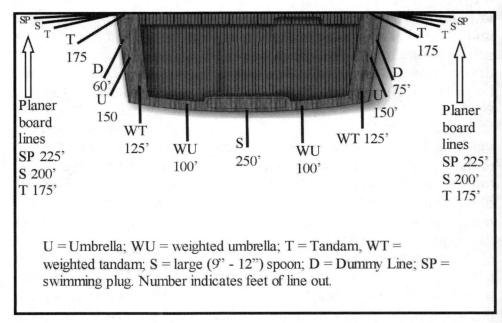

U = Umbrella; WU = weighted umbrella; T = Tandam, WT = weighted tandam; S = large (9" - 12") spoon; D = Dummy Line; SP = swimming plug. Number indicates feet of line out.

A 12 to 17 line spread like this is common to the Chesapeake charter boats during the spring trophy season, and can be applied elsewhere with the same level of success. Note: in many areas, fisheries regulations will limit the number of rods you can use.

The basic mix of umbrellas, tandem rigs, spoons, and swimming plugs makes for good offerings anywhere stripers swim. Of course, one should not plan on always setting out a specific spread, such as the one shown here, and expect success. You have to read the fish's behavior, and respond accordingly. If they keep hitting chartreuse parachutes dressed with pink shad bodies run on un-weighted tandem rigs, then swap out that white umbrella for a chartreuse one with a pink shad, and so on.

Dummy lines are also effective anywhere you're hunting for large stripers, though catching fish on a dummy line is about as unsporting as it gets. These heavy (200 pound test) lines are usually attached to cleats, not rods, run a mere 75' or so back, and are weighted down with several pounds of lead. There's a spring set in-line where it meets the cleat, and some people add a bell to the spring to indicate strikes. When a fish is hooked, the line is taken in hand over hand. It's a rig intended purely to add meat to the box, and few recreational anglers use it.

When trolling a huge spread, there are a few important things to keep in mind. Remember to keep the heavier lines shorter and in closer to the center of the boat (with the exception of dummy lines, set forward off the sides.) As the lines get lighter and longer, run them out to the sides, then from the planers. One exception: you can usually get away with one or two roof rods, run light, way back down the middle of the spread. Make sure swimming plugs are the longest lines, and that they are spread far apart, because they like to tangle other lines often. Vary the weights on your weighted lines. If, for example, your port weighted umbrella has four ounces on it, put six ounces on your starboard one. Use line counter reels, mark your line, or measure it as it goes out by counting rotations of the spool or the level-winder's motions. In any case, don't just guess at how much line you're putting back there. Keep your turns as gentle as possible, and when you hook up, make sure the nearest line(s) aren't likely to interfere with the fish.

Once you have the right gear on board and you're at the right place at the right time, you'll need to determine your trolling speed.

The bottom line is that watching your lures will help you to judge your speed the best. When they're running properly, you're going the right speed. Remember: the cooler the water is, the slower the fish are. The warmer it is, the faster the fish are. In early spring when water temperatures are 50-degrees or less, you'll want to troll as slow as your boat will go. Two or three knots is not too slow. When the water is between 50- and 60-degrees you can move it up a hair, and troll between three and four knots. Once the water rises to over 60-degrees, four to five knots is a good trolling speed. It's rare that trolling at more than five knots is necessary when fishing for stripers, and at this point, you'll start tearing up gear. Spoons spin up leaders horribly, umbrellas bend into fishing lure pretzels, and lipped plugs go sideways and break the surface. In fact, many good anglers consider three knots prime and four knots the max when trolling for stripers, and nine times out of 10, I'd agree.

One big dilemma for a lot of anglers is how to measure speed. What we're interested in, of course, is speed through the water. Speed over ground may be more or less according to the current, but speed through the water tells us exactly how much pressure is on our trolling lines and how fast our lures appear to be swimming. Most boats have paddlewheel speedos if they have a transom-mounted transducer, and these give speed through the water. They are also, however, notoriously inaccurate at slow speeds. Plus, they can get clogged with a bit of seaweed or flotsam, and give false readings. Don't trust one. Instead, place your faith in GPS. Yes, GPS does give you speed over ground. But it's a reliable number. And you can use it to easily turn speed over ground into speed through the water: simply idle into the current for a minute or two and record the speed. Then turn 180-degrees, and idle with the current. A little simple math will now tell you exactly what your speed through the water is, without any doubt or guessing. Remember that you'll have to watch your GPS as you turn and change directions, since the currents will change through the day. No GPS? You can also eliminate the influence on your speed through the water simply by trolling cross-current as opposed to into or with the current, when you have that option.

Now that you know how fast you're going, remember that as you go faster your lures will run shallower due to the increased water resistance. As you go slower, they'll run deeper. So, just how deep are they? You can use the "Rule of 5's" to get a general idea. As with everything in fishing this is not an exact science, but use the Rule of 5's as a rule of thumb when setting your lines: when trolling at five mph, with 50-lb. test line and five ounces of weight set 50' behind the boat, your lure will run about five feet under the surface. Of course, no one trolls with 50' of line out five feet below the surface. But consider the following example: If you're trolling a tandem rig tied with two five-ounce bucktails (5 x 2 = 10), and you let out 100' of line (double 50', so multiply by two again), according to the Rule of 5's it will run at about 20' below the surface (5 x 2 = 10 x 2 = 20). Naturally, the rule goes out the window the moment you introduce lipped lures or gang lures with tons of water resistance, like umbrellas. And wind, current, and sea conditions will also throw the numbers out of whack. Consider the above example, but now you're trolling at five mph against the current, which is moving at a two and a half mph. That means there's seven and a half mph of water resistance on your lines, and that tandem rig is now running at about 15' instead of 20'. To get the lure back to its intended depth, you'll either have to let out another 25' of line or slow the trolling speed. Confusing? You bet—but taking all of these factors into account and always knowing where your lures are is one of the things that separates good trollers from great ones.

Should you troll in a straight line, do zig-zags, or turn a lot? All of the above. There's nothing wrong with trolling in straight lines when you're going across long stretches of open water, collision fishing. If you're shadowing an edge or some form of structure, however, zig-zagging will allow you to take your boat over different parts and depth zones of the structure. How much you turn will depend greatly on where you are and what you're doing. (Are you fishing around a rockpile? A Channel edge?) But making turns now and again is always good, even if you turn back a moment later, because turns allow some of your lures to sink a little deeper than they're commonly

---

Bonus Trolling Tip

When the bulk of your lures are running from 20' to 30' and you see some great looking fish on the meter 10' deeper initiate a series of short turns. This will allow your lures to sink to the depth of the fish, and hopefully, generate a hook-up. You see the fish 20' or 30' deeper? Take the boat out of gear momentarily, to let the lures sink even more.

---

running. Sometimes, this is just what it takes to get a strike.

Of course, the more zig-zags and turns you do, the more likely tangles become. You need to prevent tangles by bearing in mind the placement of every lure and line in your spread from the first moment you let them over the side. Never forget that lures of similar weight and design should always be staggered, because they'll run at similar depths. If you have a port side umbrella and a starboard side umbrella, for example, run one 25' or 30' shorter than the other. Place rods rigged with shallow-running lures farther aft and out on the boat, and keep the deep runners inside and on the gunwales. If you're running planer boards, let the lightest lines out first and keep them to the outsides.

Trolling when you're targeting schoolie bass is a little different than milling around and collision fishing for the bigger fish. It's a tactic many anglers will use during the summer and early fall, when large schools of medium-sized fish are around. Lures are down-sized, from those big umbrellas and tandem parachutes to four or five inch bucktails, spoons and plugs. And a lot of in-line weight—sometimes as much as a pound—is used to get the lures down deep, where the stripers are usually holding to keep cool.

Apply this tactic when you know the fish are deep, either over a large scattered area or focused in on an item of structure. If they're holding tight to structure, obviously, stay close to it. In either case, line counter reels help a lot for this type of trolling. While spring migratory trolling rigs can be marked and set at particular lengths for more or less the entire season, when working on variable depths and structures you may need to set the lines at a different depth on each and every trip. With a line counter onboard you can let out the length that's necessary to get the weight bouncing along the bottom, reel in 10' or 12', take note of the amount of line out, and set all your rods similarly. One other interesting detail about trolling for schoolies in deep water: the fish generally seem to have a wider variety of tastes. One day white bucktails dressed with blue and pink shad body teasers are the awesome bait; the next they go untouched while green and black twister tails set the fish on fire. Do a lot of experimentation, and if you're not catching fish, don't let half an hour go by without switching something up—this is one of those situations in which you want to get innovative, maybe even a little crazy, with color patterns and choices.

One thing you'll want to pay attention to when trolling for schoolies during the warm months of the year and into the fall is the presence of birds. Usually, most folks ignore birds that are sitting on the water. But at this time of year, you should note their presence and troll in their general vicinity. Often the fish will feed at or near the surface right at daybreak or sunset, but sound whenever the sun is over the horizon. Gulls will often work in the area early on, then sit and wait as the stripers go deep to cooler waters. Although the birds sitting on the water don't mark the exact location of the fish, they do show where the fish may have been feeding earlier and provide you with one more clue as to their general location. When you come across then note the direction of the prevailing force, be it wind or current, and the direction of the bird's drift. Then, troll through the birds and continue on in the exact opposite direction.

Also take note of "dead zones" when you're targeting schoolies at this time of year. In many bays, especially the Chesapeake, a zone of anoxic (zero-oxygen) water often forms in open water, the result of too many nutrients. The nutrients cause algae blooms, which eat up all of the oxygen and then die off, leaving the anoxic water behind. It generally occurs in water 30' or deeper, from June through September (depending on conditions) as algae blooms occur.

Dead zones, while obviously a bad thing, do actually help you locate this class of fish at this time of year. Remember—the schoolies are looking for somewhere cool to hang out during the daylight hours. That means going deep. But go too deep, and they hit the anoxic water. If you can find the boarder between the anoxic water and the oxygen-rich water, and find where it intersects with structure such as a drop-off or shoal, you'll locate fish.

At first glimpse it may seem impossible to use this knowledge to your advantage—how are you supposed to know where the dead water is? Luckily, there are several ways to find out. The first is to simply putt around in an area with lots of baitfish. If you see school after school reaching down to 35' but few if any fish below 35' then you probably are looking at the anoxic water barrier. The second is to look for a thermocline, which will often be located right about at the same change. Tune up the sensitivity on your fishfinder, and look for a return that stays constant and remains at one specific depth. If you fish Chesapeake Bay, there's a third and much easier way: log on to the Internet, as mentioned earlier. Here, you can check out the location, depth and severity of the dead zone on a site-by-site basis.

Specialized Trolling

Wire lining is a specialized tactic you'll want to employ to get large lures with lots of water resistance down deep in high-current areas. Some good examples include trolling through and around the Montauk Rips in New York, Sandy Hook in New Jersey, or the CBBT in Virginia. All of these areas have one thing in common: lots of fast-moving water. Remember the Rule of 5's. Now think about what's going to happen if you're pulling a lure like an umbrella, which has a ton of water resistance, at five mph through a five mph current. To keep the lure running at 40' you'd need at least 20-ounces of lead if you let out 200' of line! Reeling in that rig will be a nightmare. If you use wire line, however, you can drop the lead by about one-third and reach the same depth. Using braid line helps, but not quite as much as wire. Call it about one-quarter less lead to reach the same depth. A couple of details about trolling with wire: first off, always keep a close eye out for kinks. A kink in the line will lead to a break-off, as soon as there's a hard tug on the line. Don't pull them tight, but push the wire back around the kink to straighten it out. Secondly, always set your drags a hair looser with wire (or braid, for that matter) than you would with mono. These lines have no stretch to absorb the impact of a solid strike, and if the drag's cranked down tight, the hook may rip free right after impact. Thirdly, always use level-wind reels when you're fishing wire lines. Otherwise, if the line piles up and snarls or makes a bird's nest, you will have a nightmare situation. Yes, experienced anglers will be okay without the level-winder. But the first time you have an inexperienced guest onboard, you'll be risking major-league problems. Other than these factors, wire-lining is really no different than other forms of heavy tackle trolling; just remember to apply it when you want to get deep, and conditions make that a tall order.

Bottom bouncing is a far more specific, specialized technique. While most forms of trolling are the best way to attack the fish when they are scattered or moving and aren't focused on a specific piece of structure (where you could target them by chumming, jigging, etc.,) bottom-bouncing is used to pluck away fish that are holding tight to bottom structure such as humps, bumps, and ledges in 20' to 50' of water. Since you'll be placing and keeping your lure along the bottom and its contours, bottom-bouncing in waters over 30' or so requires braid or wire line. Generally speaking, wire line is the best choice for bottom-bouncers regardless of depth. Not only will this line allow you to get deeper, quicker, it also has excellent sensitivity. That's important in this type of fishing, because you'll feel the take and set the hook. Either way, you'll also need stout rods that can handle five to 20 ounces of lead, depending on how much is needed to keep your lure close to the bottom. To choose a bucktail and rig it for bottom bouncing, refer back to the tackle section a few pages back.

Unlike many forms of trolling, this is an active method that requires anglers to hold and "work" the rods at all times. Rods left in holders will not catch half the fish of worked rods. In order to properly work a rod the angler must pay constant attention to both his gear and the captain, and the captain must pay constant attention to the depth finder.

Start out over level ground, far enough from the bump you're working to get all of your lines set near the bottom depth and ready to catch fish before you cross over it. Drop the line back until you feel the weight bump bottom. Lock up the reel, and maintain tension so the rig is pulled back off the bottom for at least 10 seconds. Then drop back line again, until it bounces bottom a second time. Repeat the process a third time. Now hold your rod forward so the tip is pointed towards the bow of the boat. Quickly drop the tip back while maintaining minimum tension on the line. Did you feel the weight bump bottom as the rod tip neared the stern? Perfect. If not, let out some additional line and try again. When the line's set properly you should be able to sweep the rod tip forward, then drop it back and feel the weight contact with the bottom by the time the rod is pointed aft. If the weight bumps when the rod is only half way aft, you have too much line out and need to adjust accordingly.

Now, it's time for the captain to go to work. When the boat moves over the edge of a bump he should call it out to the anglers: "The bottom's coming up from 30'. Now it's 25'. Now 22'." And so on. This way the anglers will be prepared for the rises and drops. This is important, because as soon as the depth changes you need to adjust that line or you'll either hook bottom (going up the bump) or lose contact with it (going down the bump). While crossing over the depth change, on each sweep of the rod tip the angler will have to either crank in line or drop it back, as dictated by that depth change. He should be constantly adjusting the amount of line out to keep the weight bouncing bottom at the right time, without dragging. If he does so, the stripers will smack that bucktail right when it reaches the edge of the bump.

Quite often, the fish will strike the bucktail as you're dropping the tip back. In this case the forward sweep of the rod becomes the de-facto hook-set. If you feel added resistance as you start the forward sweep you should increase your speed and strength, to get a solid hook-set. At other times, you may feel a twang on the line during the back-sweep or at the very end of the forward sweep. In either of these cases get as much tension on the line as quickly as you can and get a bend in the rod, before the fish has a chance to shake the lure free.

When applied properly, bottom-bouncing is one of the most effective methods of taking stripers around structure, period. There are a couple other factors to bear in mind, however. First off, if the structure is abrupt and snaggy, such as a wreck, bottom-bouncing will be nearly impossible because you'll snag it on nearly every pass. Secondly, give this method extra consideration when you're fishing in an area with multiple humps and bumps, but the fish have been on the move. While other forms of fishing might force you to try spot after spot until you finally find the one the fish are at, by bottom-bouncing you can troll from hump to hump and cover a lot of them in a short period of time. Then, when you find one that's productive you can stick to it.

CHAPTER SEVEN

CHUMMING

This ain't your daddy's style of chumming.

On a chilly fall morning, nothing smells as delicious as a bucket full of fresh-ground menhaden. Well, okay—maybe fresh-squeezed bloodworms, but it's a close call. Plus, chumming is a fun way to fish. You get to hold the rod in your hand and feel the strike, and then fight the fish with little or no weight squelching the action.

In its simplest form, chumming is putting ground baitfish into the water to attract predators. Chumming can also be done with grass shrimp and clams. Clams tend to be more popular as you head north along the coast, and grass shrimp are an old Chesapeake favorite. Because of the cost of each, however, they commonly take a back seat to ground menhaden in this day and age.

Chumming is usually most effective when the fish are schooled up and orienting to a particular form of structure, which can be anchored over. In most areas along the eastern seaboard that means chumming begins to be effective late in the spring or early in the summer, and increases in effectiveness through the fall. There are some exceptions, such as chumming for big migratory fish, which we'll explore later on. In fact, chumming changes with the season so much that we'll go into the particulars of each, at the end of this chapter. Regardless of the season, the need to anchor over structure and boat positioning is usually paramount when chumming. Schoolie stripers in particular will often hold tight to cover, and to effectively chum for them, you'll want to find a hump, ledge, trough or bar and anchor on the up-current side. By anchoring up-current, the tide will sweep your chum line over and around the structure.

In some cases chumming for stripers will put you in competition with a large number of boats, all putting out their own chum lines. Particularly at popular spots within shooting distance of major metropolitan areas, things can get a bit tight. There are a few ways to deal with this type of situation. First off, you can simply go somewhere else. If that's not an acceptable option, make sure you leave the dock before sunrise; few anglers will arrive before 7:00 am, and the bulk of the pack usually rolls in between 8:00 am and 8:30 am. If you're forced into joining an already-present pack of chummers, make sure you set up down-current of the pack. This will enable you to take advantage of the tail end of the packs' chum.

Chumming is usually best with a moving tide. Commonly stripers will focus on feeding during one particular slice of the tide, often the last hour or hour and a half before the tide switches. At times, they'll feed best during the hour or so when the tide is at its strongest (where in the tidal cycle this period falls depends on your location and geographical influences on the currents). And other times, they'll bite best during the first hour of the tide. They may favor the incoming, or they may favor the outgoing. And on occasion, they may even favor the slack tide. Whichever period they are feeding best on, chances are the fish will establish a pattern that holds for as long as the fish stay in the particular area, feeding on whatever bait has attracted them there. In high-traffic areas, they may simply become accustomed to feeding in chum slicks and stick around for months at a time simply because a fleet of chummers has conditioned them to do so.

So—if they may pick this slice of the tide or that one, how do you know which to focus on? It's a matter of going out a few times and identifying the pattern for yourself. If you fish two trips in a row and both times the fish are feeding at the peak of the tide, chances are they'll stick to that pattern until something forces a change: a major weather system, temperature changes, migration of bait, or any number of other factors can bring this about. As the season progresses the window of opportunity usually becomes larger and larger, and some seasons by the time November or December hits, the fish are feeding nearly through the entire cycle.

Also note that, as usual, sunrise and sunset are prime times. Often, the fish will feed just as hard in ambient light—regardless of the tide—as they will during that peak portion of the cycle. The very best time to chum, therefore, usually occurs when the peak portion of the tide coincides with either sunrise or sunset.

A lot of people think chumming is an easy gig. Toss some fish guts over the side, stick a bait on a hook, put the rod into a holder, and wait for a bite. What's the big deal? Well, anglers with this attitude will catch a few fish chumming. But you and I don't want to catch a few—we want to catch a lot of fish. And we want to catch bigger ones. If you look at chumming like a scientist instead of like a slacker, your catch rate will soar.

Tackle

Either spinning or conventional gear works well for chumming. Conventional gear does have one advantage in that rods set into the holder can be left in freespool, which often results in more hook-ups than rods set in holders with full drag on. There are a couple of spinners—Shimano's Baitrunner and Thunnus, and Penn's Liveliner—which do have a freespool function.

Generally speaking, a medium action rod with a fast action tip will work best for chumming. Six foot to seven foot is fine, but on crowded boats remember that shorter rods are usually a hair safer. Also note that slow action rods are better for anglers who will leave their rods sitting in the rodholders, since they will absorb some of the tension when a fish strikes. Fast action is better for those who constantly hold their rod and are ready to set the hook on a moment's notice. In either case, they should be rigged up with 12- to 17-pound test monofilament. If you expect monster stripers, move it up to 20-pound test. Going much beyond that is overkill.

The chumming rig itself is extraordinarily simple: three to four feet of fluorocarbon leader with a 5/0 – 7/0 hook on one end, and a loop or swivel on the other. I personally prefer a Gamakatsu Octopus or an Owner Needle Point SSW. You'll note that these hooks have the eye bent back, which is intended for snelling. I don't snell these hooks and I won't pretend to know why they work so well for chumming when tied on with a fisherman's knot instead of being snelled—but they do. What about circle hooks? Aren't they the best thing since sliced bread? I don't like them for one simple reason:

I catch more fish with the aforementioned hooks. That said, some extremely good anglers I know use circle hooks exclusively. Nearly all of them, however, are offset. Many people don't realize that offset circle hooks—which do seem more effective than those that are not offset—will gut-hook a fish every bit as much as a regular J-hook. The vast majority of the circle hooks on the market are in fact offset, and in some places it can actually be very difficult to come by those that aren't offset.

After that little diatribe, let's make one thing clear: chumming is not a good tactic for catch-and-release angling. No matter what you do you will gut-hook some fish when chumming, and if you don't plan on harvesting fish, simply try some other method. If, on the other hand, you do intend to put fish in the box, why not use the most effective hooks even if they do lead to more gut-hookings? All that's well and fine until you start catching lots of throw-backs, right? Then, those gut-hooked fish you release are a terrible shame. That's why any angler worth his salt will either switch to a different method of fishing or change locations, when a large percentage of the chum-caught fish are shorts.

Tactics

Though chumming seems simple, it's the little details you need to pay attention to if you want to out-catch the next fellow. The chum itself, for example. Are you going to get fresh menhaden and grind it on the spot? Purchase pre-ground chum, frozen in a bucket? Or pre-ground chum frozen in a mesh bag?

While it's important to use fresh bunker for your baits whenever possible—it absolutely, positively, will draw more strikes than frozen menhaden—it doesn't seem terribly imperative that the chum be fresh. So, it makes a lot of sense to opt for frozen chum. It can be hung in the water where it will release a steady, constant flow, as it thaws. And as most of you probably already know, the key to a good chum slick is not volume, it is consistency.

If this is the case, why do so many charter boats and professionals grind chum on the spot? Remember that they usually have professional mates onboard to keep the flow steady. Amid the mayhem of multiple hook-ups, scrambling for new baits, and netting fish, there's always a seasoned pro keeping the slick going. For most recreational anglers, the seasoned crewmember doesn't exist and as a result, breaks in the chum line will occur. You can't tell your brother-in-law to keep the chum line steady, and expect him to know what to do or to do it effectively. For this reason, grinding fresh on-site will do most recreational anglers more harm than good.

Still, there are several forms of chum to choose from. Many people up and down the coast have purchased chum "logs" which come in a red net mesh bag. If you'd like to watch your chum log float away after 15 minutes of fishing, go right ahead and use that mesh bag. If you intend on fishing seriously, rip it off the log and drop the chum into a heavy-duty nylon mesh bag. You'll see these bags at any tackle shop, and they will do the job. Unfortunately, unless you're willing to spend half an hour with a scrub brush and a hose, they will also stink to the extreme a week after a fishing trip. That's why savvy chummers get the frozen stuff that's sold in one-gallon plastic buckets. You can cut nickel-sized holes in these buckets, tie them off to a cleat, and when the day is over either toss them or save the holy bucket for next time. When you get your next chum bucket, invert it and slide the bucket off of the frozen chum. Then simply slide the chum into the old, pre-cut bucket. When using plastic buckets there is, however, one more thing to be aware of. In heavy seas the top may pop off, allowing your chum to float away. Prevent this problem by cutting a hole in the top and one near it in the side of the bucket. Then tie your line off through both of these holes, so the top of the bucket is always held securely in place. And don't trust a single piece of kite string to hold the bucket to the boat. Use clothesline or a similar rope that won't break when a gallon of chum gets yanked around by a three foot wave.

How much chum is necessary? A hard-frozen one gallon bucket will last between two and four hours. Water temperature and sea conditions will have a dramatic effect on the chum's longevity. In heavy seas the bucket will constantly be yanked and jerked, and the chum will flow out rather quickly. In calm seas it may just sit there, failing to disburse enough to have a real effect. You can influence the lifespan of your chum bucket, however, by tying it on a longer or shorter leash. Short lines will keep the bucket dancing near the surface, throwing chum as liberally as possible. Longer lines will allow the bucket to sink below the surface, dampening the effect of the waves.

In some cases—spring trophy chumming, or chumming on a bright day in hot, calm conditions for example—you may want your chum to be at or near the bottom, instead of up at the surface. When this is the case, it's time to break out the sinking chum pot. You can purchase small wire cage-like chum pots at most tackle shops, and these do work well. If your chum is frozen you may have to hack off chunks to fill the sinking pot, but that's easy enough to do. Another trick is to fill a plastic film container with chum, poke a few holes in it, and use a swivel clip to secure it to your line, a few feet above the bait. Sand balls are another chum-sinking method; simply carry a bucket of sand aboard with you, and mold the sand around chum balls before tossing it over the side. This method works great but I don't recommend it to those who care about the looks of their boat, because the sand gets everywhere and scratches up fiberglass gel coat in no time. Brown-bagging is a better way to get some chum down fast, and all you need to do to be prepared for this task is to always carry a pack of brown paper lunch bags aboard your boat. When you need to get that chum deep, rig up a line with a heavy weight and a large hook. Put a handful of chum into a paper bag, twist the top shut, run the hook through it a couple times, then lower it to the bottom. Wait 10 or 12 seconds, then give it a good, sharp yank and the paper bag will rip right open, disbursing the chum low in the water column.

Chum slicks can also be enhanced with a number of commercial products. Some anglers swear by adding dog food, or dried chum sold commercially. Others put glitter in the chum. And some innovative angler figured out that he could smash up the shells from his scrambled egg breakfast, mix them into the chum, and add nice flashy white bits to the chum slick. Maybe this stuff helps, but the only additive you can really count on is bunker oil. Menhaden milk, a mixture based on bunker oil, also does help. This stuff remains at the surface and dissipates quickly when the tide's running, so you need to either add it to the chum bucket regularly or use an IV drip bag to keep it flowing steadily. Soaking your baits in the stuff before lowering them over the side definitely doesn't hurt, either.

More about those baits—how you cut them will have a significant impact on how full your cooler is at the end of the day. Both fillets and chunks will be effective. Interestingly, from New Jersey north a lot of anglers like to use the heads of the bunker as bait, while most anglers south of the Mason Dixon line toss the head overboard. When you cut fillets, always put your hook in through the meat and out through the skin, one time. Doubling the bait back on the hook often causes the bait to spin, which in turn leads to tangles. Plus, they won't get hit as often because they look unnatural. Have you ever seen a piece of chopped fish spin in circles, of its own volition? Neither have the stripers.

Chunks should either be hooked once through the back, or in the case of dice, threaded onto the hook. What's a dice? When stripers get finicky and poke and pick at baits but they just won't seem to eat the darn things, try cutting your fillets into little dice-sized pieces. Then thread them onto your hook, one by one, until the entire shank is covered. Often the largest, most wary fish will eat a dice bait when it only mouths larger baits.

Regardless of what type of bait you cut, a chunk of guts is always a good thing. Menhaden gut are, of course, rather weak and slimy. Goop them over your hook, and they'll fall off in a matter of seconds. But there is one small, hard knobby thing in the middle of the guts—some call it a gizzard, but heck if I know what it actually is—and if you can get your hook through it most of the slimy stuff stays along for the ride. And yes, the stripers like it a lot.

Regardless of the size or shape of the bait you are using, before you deploy your offering lower it a foot or two into the water

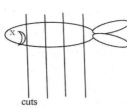

cuts

Step 1: Make 1" to 2" wide cuts, all the way through body. Discard head and tail (northern anglers like using the head, especially for large fish.)

cut

Step 2: Turn chunks on their side, and cut next to spine. You'll get two baits per chunk.

Gut glob

Step 3: Thread the chunk onto the hook going in through the meat side and out through the skin side, in the back (not rib cage) section of the bait. To add appeal, hang a glob of menhaden guts on the hook point.

Alternate: Thred on the entire chunk; go in through one side of the back and out the other. (Use when prolific undersize fish are a nusiance.)

Properly cut and rigged menhaden baits, for use when chumming.

and sweep your rod tip forward, to get a look at how that bait will act when there's some water pressure on it. If the bait spins, rip it off and start over. Nothing's worse than a spinning bait, and if you've ever pulled up a twisted, tangled mess while chumming, there's a good chance a spinning bait was the culprit. (Allowing the bait to free-fall is responsible for many tangles, too. If your rig falls so fast that the bait wraps around your main line above the swivel connection, you'll have a guaranteed mess. Try slowing it down a hair as it falls, to solve the problem.)

Unlike the chum itself, the fresh versus frozen debate does

have import when you're talking about baits. There's no doubt that much of the time, fresh baits will out-fish frozen ones. And baits that have been frozen, thawed, then frozen again are nearly worthless. You have once-frozen baits left over at the end of the day? Either throw them away or use them for crab bait, but don't cheap-out if you hope to catch good numbers of rockfish.

Many anglers feel that clam or crab baits are the way to go, when chumming. No doubt, these are effective baits at times. They seem particularly good when there's a crowd of boats chumming in a particular area, and the fish have a lot of offerings to choose from. And these alternative baits will often out-fish frozen menhaden baits. But generally speaking, good fresh menhaden will out-fish all of the other bait options in a menhaden chum slick. If you can get enough clams to chum them, by all means, use clam baits. Same goes for grass shrimp, which used to be chummed extensively in the northern areas of the Chesapeake. But when ground fish is in the slick, it seems like that's what the fish usually want to feed on.

Spring Chumming

Spring chumming is unique when compared to chumming the rest of the year. Why? Remember that the fish are migrating. They don't have much interest in sticking around in one place, and a chum line is not enough to hold them in one spot. Instead, you have to remember that the best you can do is tempt the fish into taking a pass or two through the area. The big cows like to scavenge free meals when possible, and will eat fresh menhaden baits off the bottom simply because it's easy to do so.

This makes boat positioning a lot easier than it will be the rest of the year. For once, being located right over the edge, hump or bump isn't all that important—the fish aren't staging where you're setting up, anyway. Instead, simply look for featureless bottoms that you know the fish will be migrating through. A perfect example of such a spot—and my own personal favorite for spring trophy fishing—is the Love Point mud flat, just above the Chesapeake Bay Bridge. The muddy bottom here ranges between 30' and 50' and doesn't have any abrupt changes. But if you sink a chum pot to the bottom and set out your baits, migratory fish will drop down and chomp on them. Interestingly, these fish will only feed in this way during certain slices of the tide.

In chapter 2 when discussing tide and fish behavior in specific, we learned that catch records going back well over a decade, which included each and every trophy striper caught by my boat, my father's and several friends, proved an astonishing pattern: 80-percent of the trophies caught during the migratory period came during a one and a half hour slice of the tide. 10-percent of the remaining fish were caught in the following hour and the oddball ten percent came to the hook at sunrise or sunset, which (I'm sure you already know) is a time of active feeding for the fish in any case. We also learned that the last 90 minutes of the tidal cycle was that red-hot time period. The incoming tide beat out the outgoing by a slight margin, but both were productive. The first 60 minutes of the following tidal cycle accounts for the other active, but much slower, productive period.

Of course, other variables mentioned earlier in this book did have an effect on the fishing; rainfall and water clarity made spring chumming more or less effective when considering the overall number of fish caught during any given time frame. In essence, more rainfall in the spring translated into fewer trophies caught. Clarity helps but is not imperative. Clear water during springs of heavy fresh flow are not as productive as cloudy water during springs of less fresh flow, for example.

It's important to note that fish caught using this technique are behaving in a different way than those being caught by trollers, and the "hot" area for trolling at any given time will not necessarily be a good choice for chumming. Conversely, trollers in a particular location may be catching a skunk when chummers are tearing the fish up.

Since the window of opportunity is so small, this method of fishing is bit more risky than trolling. You have to chose your spot, and remain dedicated to it through the hot period of the tide. So—why chum in the first place, if trolling is less risky and has a higher chance of success? Trolling means heavy gear, broomstick like rods, and gobs of lead. Often, 30-pound fish are barely detectable on umbrella rigs, Billy Bars, and other mega-baits that are so effective in the early spring. But chumming allows you to catch those big fish on extremely light gear. A 12-pound rig is perfect for this type of fishing, and if you hook into a 40-inch or larger fish, you'll have the fight of a lifetime. For many anglers, myself included, this opportunity alone makes the trade-off worthwhile.

Luckily, sharp anglers know that if the first spot you choose doesn't produce, all is not necessarily lost. You can run to another spot which experiences the tidal flow later than the one you started at, and "chase" the tide to get in a couple of shots at different locations throughout the course of a day. Depending on your starting point, if you cruise at 30-mph or better you can usually find a second spot that takes a 20 minute or so run to get to, but gains you an hour on the tidal flow—generating another 40 minutes of productive fishing time. Of course, the exact timing will vary quite a bit depending on your location and the strength of the tidal flow there. So pore over the tide tables before you fish, and make up a game plan accordingly.

Note that virtually every fish you hook when chumming in the migratory period will come from baits set dead on the bottom. Jigged baits will go untouched and drifted baits will be ignored. Again, this runs counter to traditional theory; when trolling in the spring the many of your fish come on lines run relatively high in the water column. So what gives? The fish you catch chumming at this time of year are feeding in a way that is different than the way they are acting when you catch them on the troll. I can't tell you why—that's a question for the scientists—but it means you'll have to act accordingly if you want to hook them. You'll need to sink your chum pot to the bottom, hung just a foot or two above mud so the motion of the boat helps shake out the chum. Baits should be large, either chunks or fillets the size of your fist, to help get that smell out there and tempt those trophy cows. Rigs for use in the spring should be made with four feet of fluorocarbon 30-lb. test leader terminating with a 6/0 hook. Gamak-atsu Octopus and Owner Cutting Point hooks are my favorites for the job. Rig an egg sinker above your leader (stagger different rigs with different sized weights, so they sit on bottom at different distances behind the boat,) and connect the main line to the leader with a ball-bearing swivel.

Rods left in holders (both for bottom and balloon rigs—more on balloon rigs soon) should be left on freespool with the clicker on, so that fish can take line freely. If your rod doesn't have a freespool function you can bend a metal twist-tie around the base of the rod or the reel seat, then bend a hook into the end. Set your line in the hook and it will hold the line until a fish comes along and pulls it free.

Held rods should be kept in freespool (or open bailer) at all times, with a finger keeping the line from spilling out. The moment you detect the slightest sign of a bite, drop the tip and feed the fish line. While you will sometimes get that freight-train strike, even the biggest trophies often slurp in the bait so gently that you can barely detect it. Allow these fish plenty of time to eat—between five and 10 seconds before you tighten up the line and attempt a hook-set is appropriate. Remember that these big spawners are a lot smarter than the schoolie bass which will often eat just about anything with abandon. If the fish feel a jerk on the line, too much resistance, or if they taste a frozen bait, they're just as likely to spit it out as they are to swallow it.

Ready for the exception to the spring chumming rigging rules? Whole menhaden rigged to look alive, suspended 10' to 25' below the surface with a balloon, will also catch fish when spring chum-ming—even as chunks suspended right next to them go untouched. Rigging dead-as-a-doornail menhaden to look lively is easier said than done. When you do it properly, however, these rigged baits look quite good in the water and can also be used for jigging, drifting, or even trolling and mooching. Here's how to set them up.

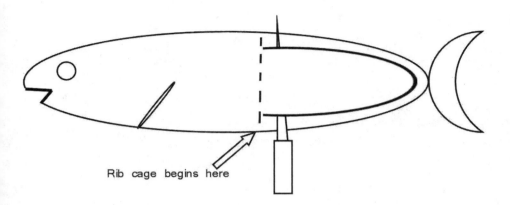

Rib cage begins here

STEP 1: Using a sharp fillet knife, fillet the fish halfway up on both sides, without cutting the fillet free of the body. Start at the tail, and separate the meat and skin from the backbone up until you reach the rib cage. For those familiar with offshore rigging, this is just like preparing a split-tail mullet.

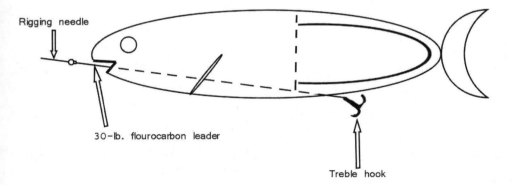

Rigging needle

30–lb. flourocarbon leader

Treble hook

STEP 2: Tie a foot-long section of fluorocarbon leader to a treble hook on one end, and a rigging needle on the other. Run the needle in at the end of the cut you made, near the rib cage, on the bottom of the fish. Push it out through the fish's mouth.

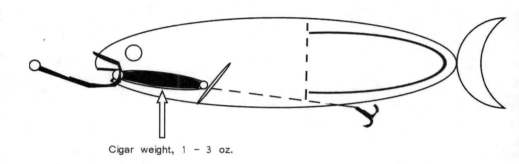

Cigar weight, 1 - 3 oz.

STEP 3: Tie the end of the leader to a one, two or three ounce torpedo-style weight. Then push the weight into the fish's mouth. Run a short-shank 4/0 to 6/0 hook (depending on the size of the bait) through the lower jaw of the fish, through the eye of the weight, then through the upper jaw, so the hook pins the weight in place. Use a pair of pliers to squeeze the eye of the weight closed a bit, so the hook can't back out through it.

Lazy man's method: Instead of running a rigging needle through the fish, simply tie a six-inch leader to the eye or shank of the hook, string it along the outside of the fish, and place one of the three tines of the treble in the fish's back or underbelly. This works fairly well for a short period of time, but the treble usually works its way free of the menhaden sooner or later, and wraps on the main line or gets stuck who-knows-where on the fish and may be ineffective when the striper grabs the aft end of the menhaden. If you rig them with the leader on the outside of the fish, be sure to check your baits every half-hour to prevent this problem.

Once the bait is rigged up, tie your leader to the hook in its mouth and you're ready to lower it away. Use a rubber band to secure additional weight to the line where the leader meets your swivel, if it's necessary to keep the bait down in a moving current. Strip out enough line to set the bait just below the surface, 25' down or at mid-depth as desired, (one bait set at each is the prime set-up,) then tie a regular balloon around the line using an overhand knot.

The balloon will act as a bobber, keeping your bait at the proper depth while bobbing up and down on the waves, imparting some action to the bait. As one might suspect, this rig is by far more effective when there's a chop on the water. If it's unusually calm out, you can boost its effectiveness by cranking in 20' or so feet of line then dropping the rig back, every so often.

When you reel the rig up and the balloon hits the eye of your rod, the line will pass right through it (unlike a bobber). If a fish drags it under, often the balloon will pop anyway, allowing you to reel in the line unencumbered. Either way, the balloon shouldn't interfere with bringing your line in. Note that when fish take this rig you'll commonly see the balloon slide sideways across the surface, as opposed to going under.

There are a few other interesting tidbits about spring trophy chumming. For one, nearly all of the fish you catch will be big ones. It's rare to find a fish under 30" using this tactic in the early spring, and the majority of the fish will run from 32" to 42". It's also a relatively "clean" fishery. Few big cow females come to the hook using these tactics, and most of the fish you catch are either very large males or post-spawn females. Unlike those caught while trolling, checking the gut of fish caught spring chumming will turn up very little roe, perhaps one time for every six or seven fish (as opposed to 40 or 50 percent of trolled fish.) Also note that this should be viewed purely as a harvest method. If you want to catch and release fish, don't use these tactics, because a large percentage of the fish will be gut-hooked. As mentioned earlier, I don't particularly like circle hooks for this fishing method and since I haven't tested their reliability in this regard, can't speak to their effectiveness versus the hooks I regularly use. Again, however, it should be stressed that fishing with offset circle hooks will not eliminate the gut-hooking problem. So save spring chumming trips for those times that you intend to harvest a fish or two.

Summer Chumming

Once water temperatures rise, stripers will start to school up and focus on specific areas, establish more stable feeding patterns, and feed with a little more interest. The late spring/early summer months usually mean good action, until the water rises to above the upper-70's in southern areas; at this point, fishing often becomes tough again. Northern climates, however, with their cooler summer water, will enjoy good fishing. But remember—these fish are no longer in a migratory pattern. Throw everything you know about spring chumming out the window, and start over again.

As the stripers form pods and the pods join to form schools, the fish will start to orient to structure. Humps and bumps, channel edges, and drop-offs become their gathering places, and the position of your boat will be a make-or-break factor.

Once you locate a structural item that's holding fish, anchor on the up-current side. By anchoring up-current, the tide will sweep your chum line over and around the structure. Make sure your boat is literally right on the edge—when the surrounding depth is 35', the hump comes up to 15', and your depth finder reads 25', you know you're in the zone.

Okay, you've got the anchor down, there's chum hanging over the side of the boat, and you're ready to fish. This is how most people chum, and it does work: They hang a chum bag or bucket at the surface, and set out a line with little or no weight, 30' to 50' back. A second line goes out with half an ounce of weight, and is set the same distance back just below surface. A third one gets an ounce and hangs at mid-depth, and a forth line is rigged with enough weight to stay at or near the bottom. All four rods are placed in holders, and the anglers sit while they wait for a strike. This is simple and somewhat effective—but very lazy—fishing. If you want to boost your catch rate considerably, use these two tricks: first, do not set your surface line. Instead, put your reel in freespool, and dangle the bait right next to the chum bucket. Now give a few tugs on the bucket's rope, so a nice cloud of chum flows out. At the same time, release all tension on your surface bait and allow it to drift back and sink naturally, in that cloud of chum. Strip line from your reel and keep everything slack, so the bait is not pulled out of the chum cloud by tension from the line. Watch the slack line as your bait moves back, and when you see the line jerk or suddenly change direction, set the hook. If nothing strikes after you've drifted the bait back 100' or so, reel in and start over. Any day of the week you'll catch a lot more fish using this method than you will with a surface baited rod in the holder.

Trick number two: as you probably know already, larger fish will often come from baits set on bottom. You should also know that in order to effectively fish the bottom you'll need weight, and if you set a rod untended in the holder, you won't be able to feed fish line upon the initial bite. Fish that strike the bottom line are therefore likely to feel that weight and dump the bait. You can fix this problem, however, at least when the current is moving. Use an egg sinker, larger than necessary to hold bottom. Even in low current use at least three ounces for this purpose, and usually four is better. Set it on bottom, then let out line as you sweep your rod tip forward. Keeping minimum tension on the line, let your tip go back slowly. The current will pull on your bait, and take line out through the egg sinker. (This is why you want an oversized weight; smaller sinkers will get pushed back by the current.) Repeat the process two or three times until you have let 10' to 15' of line out through the egg sinker. This extra line out beyond the sinker allows the fish to swim for several seconds before feeling any unusual resistance.

Rigging and baiting for summer chumming is an exercise in simplicity. Just use a four to five foot length of 30-lb. test leader with a 5/0 or 6/0 hook, tied off on a ball-bearing swivel or terminating in a loop knot. Spinning or conventional gear in the 10- to 20-lb. class matches up well against most of the stripers you'll encounter when chumming scoolie fish.

Note that while the tide is important at this time of year, it's not nearly as make-or-break as it is for spring chumming. Stripers will tend to establish patterns around the tide that commonly revolve around the change. Some seasons the last part of one tide or another is best, others the first part of one tide or another is best. Most commonly the last of the incoming is a good time to fish, but it can vary from season to season and place to place. At this time of year, light levels and water temperature grow in importance. Stripers are a tad light-sensitive, and will shy away from feeding at the surface on bright, sunny, hot days. At times like these concentrate more of your efforts lower in the water column. Conversely, when it's gray and cloudy out make sure you have a line or two at the surface.

If water temperatures in your area creep into the upper 70's or the 80's, look for the fish to be hanging deep during daylight hours. Commonly summer fish will prowl in the upper 20's or lower 30's. Those areas that see "dead zones" of deep water will be affected even more dramatically. Dead zones are areas of anoxic water which form from over-nitrification during the warmer months of the year. They have oxygen levels so low that fish can't survive in them. Often, they start around 30' and affect deeper water. This puts the stripers in a bind—they want to go deep to reach cooler temperatures, yet they can't go any deeper than the beginning of the dead zone. In these conditions, the trick is to locate the beginning of the dead water and fish on structure that rises just a few feet above it. If, for example, 30' is the breaking point, and you can find a hump that comes up to 26' or 28' and is surrounded by 40' or deeper water, you have a spot with good potential.

Fall Chumming

Most seasons, chumming is at its best in the fall. Particularly in areas that see a lot of bluefish, cooler temperatures which force their migration mean you can focus solely on the bass—and at this time of year, the bass are usually on the feed. Hits often come for much larger segments of the tide, and sometimes the stripers will feed clear through the cycle.

The tactics you use for fall chumming should be more or less identical to those used for summer chumming. Pay slightly more attention to getting lines higher up in the water column, since stripers are apt to be feeding at or near the surface during this season, but remember that larger fish often shadow schools of smaller ones by hanging a little deeper than the main body of fish. If you want to focus on lunkers, keep a line or two down deep.

Also note that during the fall, young of the year peanut bunker (and mullet, in areas close to the beach) are migrating out of the creeks, bays, and inlets. If you can fill your livewell by throwing a cast net at first light, you have an excellent chance of taking more fish than competitors with near-by chum lines. Fish the live baits as you would chunks of menhaden, but lip-hook them with short-shank hooks. This tactic works very well once the bluefish have moved out but remember that if they're still in the area, they'll chop the rear end off of most of the live baits you deploy in a chum line.

There are a few more details you should keep in mind when chumming, regardless of the season. First off, use monofilament, not superline or braid. Superlines are great for some situations, but chumming is not one of them. For some reason superlines change the sink rate, and seem to cut the water better and sink faster than monofilament. They also have greatly increased sensitivity, and although this means you feel the fish bite sooner than you would with mono, it means they feel you sooner, too. Try fishing them side by side and you'll notice that mono will out-chum braid, every time.

Casting chum rigs is another mistake you see people make all the time—there's no better way to quickly get your bait far away from the chum line (and the fish) than casting! Plus, casting increases the likelihood that the bait will wrap around the main line and cause a tangle. Instead, chumming rigs should be lowered over the side and controlled as they drop. You want to stagger the distance between your lines? Good thinking. Instead of casting, vary the sizes of the weights you use and the current will do the job for you.

Also remember that throughout the season, getting an early

start is incredibly important. The bite is often strongest right as the sun breaks the horizon, and if you're fishing in a popular area it can be very important to beat the other boats to get a prime position on the hotspot. If you can't get out early, stay late. The last hour of sunlight is another time the stripers feed heavily, and again, the competition will be thinner.

CHAPTER EIGHT

LIVE BAITING

When the fish won't bite, live bait is often the ticket to a bent rod.

It's hard to beat live bait; a kicking bunker or a wiggling eel will tempt the wisest of the striped bass. Livies can be fished with or without weight, allowing you to apply the tactic whether the water is deep or shallow and the currents are strong or weak. And live baits allow you to match the hatch with exact precision, increasing your effectiveness when the stripers are focused on a specific prey.

One of the best times to apply live baiting tactics is when there's a lot of competition. Most people won't put in the time or effort necessary to catch a bucket full of bait-size spot, or throw a cast net over a livewell worth of bunker. And most livies (except eels) aren't stocked by most tackle shops. That means that if you do go the extra mile, you can out-fish everyone else.

Of course, as with anything, there are drawbacks to this form of fishing, as well. Beyond the time and effort necessary to catch and keep live baits alive, the biggest problems will usually arise when bluefish are present in good numbers. Often, the blues will chop your baits in half over and over again, until the livewell's empty. There's really no way to combat this problem, so if an area is infested with bluefish, it's probably better to use a different tactic.

Tackle

Rigs for live baiting, be it with eels or baitfish, are commonly similar to those used for chumming except they have short-shank hooks. Leaders made with 20- 30-lb. test are plenty heavy when live baiting unless you're using 8" herring to catch 50" fish, and when fishing with small livies, remember that lighter leader will allow the bait more freedom of movement. Another difference between chumming and live bait rigs: instead of using an egg sinker many anglers will simply use an in-line torpedo weight, and some opt for fishfinder-

This striper fell for a live peanut bunker...it was his last meal.

style rigs. And finally, when live baiting with small peanut bunker it's usually necessary to use very thin hooks, as opposed to the stouter hooks used for other types of fishing. Otherwise, their delicate jaw may be split and the bait will be ruined. 2/0's rigged up on 20-lb. test is a good size to stick with, and since you commonly fish peanuts in relatively shallow water (more on this later) a half-ounce of lead will usually suffice.

Rods and reels vary depending on personal preference. 10 to 20-lb. spinning or conventional gear works well, but you may want to up-size a bit if really big cows are in town. Rods should generally have relatively fast action for live baiting, for solid hook-sets. Short boat rods are convenient and the usual drawback of squelched casting ability is a moot point, since you don't need to cast live baits but instead will commonly drift or fish them at anchor.

If you're live baiting with fish, such as bunker, spot, or perch, one item you'll need onboard is a livewell. Most modern boats are equipped with decent livewells, but there are tricks you can use to make them better. If yours is loaded up and would benefit from more water flow (or if the pump dies, and leaves you in a lurch,) turn your raw water washdown hose on and hang it into the well so it sprays constantly. You may also want to add oxygen injection. This is a relatively expensive proposition—you'll have to buy and install the injection system. The cheapest on the market runs about $100, and you could easily spend $400 to $500 (or more if you pay someone else to install it) on an infusion system.

Add-on livewells used to retrofit boats built without bait-hauling abilities are not cheap, either. A 30-gallon model will cost several hundred dollars for the tank, and another hundred or so for a pump, hose, and wiring materials. What about the old five-gallon bucket method? Truth be told, you can make it work, even for delicate baits like peanut bunker. The first and most important thing is to not overload the buckets with fish. When dealing with four to five inch baits keep no more than two per gallon of water, and when dealing with larger baits, one per gallon of water. You'll have to pay constant attention to the baits, and remember to change at least one gallon of water out of each bucket every 10 minutes. For this reason, it's best to have an extra bucket on hand at all times, so you can scoop and fill as needed. Adding a battery operated aerator will help, but these units do not have a massive effect. Even with one hanging in the bucket you'll need to change the water every 15 to 20 minutes.

Once the fish are on the hook, there are a few tricks you can use to keep them living longer. While "lip-hooking" the fish is one of two effective ways to rig the live fish (more on this soon,) you should be careful to run the hook through the fish's nostrils, instead of through the upper and lower jaws. This will allow it to push water through its gills and breath easier. Refrain from casting live baits as much as possible, as this does take a serious toll on them. And when moving from spot to spot, even if its just for a few seconds, keep any hooked live baits in a bucket of water.

Keeping eels is much different—and thankfully, much easier—than keeping baitfish in good condition. Forget the livewell; it's nearly impossible to catch a healthy eel in a livewell and once you do catch it, good luck getting that slimy little fellow onto the hook. Instead, keep your eels in a rectangular Tupperware container. Then, place the container of eels on ice in your cooler or fishbox, where they'll chill down. Like crabs, the eels will go into a pseudo-hibernation mode in a matter of minutes. When you're ready to fish, grasp an eel with a paper towel—even when they're sleeping it's tough to hold one of these slime balls bare-handed—and insert the hook in through the lower jaw and out through the upper jaw. Within seconds of being lowered over the side the eel will warm up and spring back to life.

Between drifts or when traveling to new spots, it's necessary to take special care with the eel on your hook. Let it rest on the deck or hang over the side, and the eel will often twist itself into knots. A few minutes later, your leader will be in knots as well. Instead, carry a small one-gallon bucket for each of the anglers onboard. When it's time to move, put about one inch of water into the bucket, and dangle the eel into it with just enough slack that the eel rests on the bottom of the bucket. Don't put more than one rigged eel in each bucket, or they'll twist the leaders around each other in seconds.

As with other live baits, most anglers will fish eels on short-shank hooks tied to a 4' leader in the 30-lb test range, which is weighted down with either a torpedo or egg sinker. Don't get shy about adding plenty of weight, because stripers will usually take eels from dead on bottom. If your bait isn't getting all the way down there the chances are it won't be hit.

Tactics
Peanut Bunker, Spot, and White Perch

Each of these fish make good live baits, but some are better than others. Peanut bunker are usually the best, especially during the fall months when stripers are waiting to ambush them as they migrate out of creeks, rivers and bays. Spot are an excellent live bait for use in the spring and summer when bunker of good bait size can be tough to acquire, and perch are more or less a back-up to these more tempting fish. We should note at this point that traditionally, many other fish (such as fluke, croaker, and weakfish) have also been used as live baits. But these days, it's against the regulations to bait with them in most areas, if for no other reason than because minimum size limits preclude their use.

Fishing live baits is almost always most effectively done on the drift, unless you have located a specific shelf or hump that's stacked thick with fish and which you can anchor over. Rough weather may also mean anchoring is a good move, if the drift is so fast you can hardly get a bait down before blowing off the spot. Even then, pin-point anchoring may be necessary to get the boat over the fish and if you get it the least little bit off you won't catch a thing. Always consider your options carefully, before dropping the big hook.

The exceptions to this rule: when you're night fishing, and sometimes when fishing in inlets. In the night fishing scenario, if you're working a light-line or bridge pilings near light-lines, anchoring is usually the better choice since it will allow you to keep your baits in the appropriate strike zone. And in inlets, where specific notches or rocks in a jetty may hold special attraction to the rockfish, anchoring may be necessary to place and keep your bait in the strike zone. Remember—along inlet jetties stripers may orient to a specific irregularity very tightly, and your bait has to be practically in their face to draw a strike. You may be able to cast slightly up-current of the feature (so close that your offering nearly kisses the rocks) and let the current swept it back towards the fish, or you may need to get up-current of the fish-attracting feature and drift your bait back to it. Since anchoring represents a pretty significant investment of your fishing time,

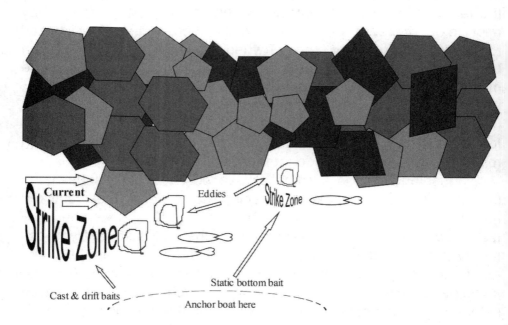

Where you find notches or loose rocks in an inlet jetty, stripers will often move in. Whenever possible anchor so you can offer two baits to two strike zones—with differing presentations—at the same time.

try to identify a spot that offers you both opportunities. One where you can cast an offering up-current and let it drift through strike zone number one, while a weighted live bait can be positioned so it drifts back to a second strike zone, and remains there. If the fish are feeding up top or mid-depth, they'll have both your cast and drifted bait to consider. And if they're hugging close to the bottom, the static bait should do the trick.

Whether adrift or not, livies are usually going to prove more effective when fished on bottom. At times, however, they'll be a real killer when simply live-lined (allowed to swim freely) with no additional weight. This is an excellent option in the appropriate conditions, since it allows the striper to take the live bait without feeling much resistance on the line. It will be much less likely to dump the bait, and usually a live-lined fish that gets attacked gets eaten all the way down. So, what are the appropriate conditions? Slow water is one; little or no current combined with little or no drift allows the baits to swim where they please. Whenever stripers are feeding at or near the surface, live lining like this works well. Night fishing around light lines is another situation in which weight-free live lining shines. And when you're fishing around a balled school of baitfish (and you believe stripers are prowling the periphery) it's another good chance to apply the tactic.

In some areas at some times, it may even be possible to live line baits at or near the bottom without any weight. You can "encourage" the baitfish to head down towards the bottom by hooking it through the back, just behind the dorsal fin—the second of the two effective ways to hook live baits. Note that any significant water resistance due to either current or drifting will make baits rigged like this appear unnatural. There aren't many bunker that learn to swim backwards through the water, and stripers know it. The rest of the time you'll be better off by hooking the baitfish through the head, with going through the nostrils being the least-damaging way to hook the baitfish.

While live baiting fish like these is an effective tactic just about any time, there is one particular exception to note: spring migratory

Bonus Factoid
Live-Baiting Tip

Whenever you lower a perch, spot, or similar baitfish over the side, use a pair of scissors to snip off one pectoral fin. It'll make the bait- fish struggle in circles, and appear nice and injured when big old Mr. Bass comes along.

stripers which are on the move will often take a cut dead bait before attacking a live fish. Perhaps it's laziness, but for whatever reason the fish don't want to engage in a chase. I know this sounds com- pletely bizarre, and if someone told me this a few years back I would have laughed in their face. But after fishing live six to nine inch her- ring next to cut baits and seeing the cut baits get all the action time and time again, I'm convinced—those big cows just aren't interested in chasing frisky baitfish when they're in migration mode. So, when targeting these fish bear in mind that cut bait may be more effective than live baits.

During the early fall, when small, young-of-the-year "peanut" bunker have grown to three to five inches and are migrating out of creeks, rivers, and small bays, live baiting is a particularly effective method. Stripers in the 14" to 30" class know this migration is about to take place, and they'll be planning to take advantage of it. Tribu- tary river mouths feeding bays like the Chesapeake, rivers like the Hudson, and sounds like Long Island, will stack up with fish looking for easy meals. The exact timing varies up and down the coast and will change from season to season depending on the weather, but this migration usually starts some time in September and is over by some time in late October. As it occurs, you'll find the fish hanging at channel drop-offs and the ends of points running out into the body of water. They'll be relatively shallow, commonly in 12' to 20' of water and sometimes even less. Locate these fish, put a live peanut bunker in front of them, and you're about to hook up.

Of course, you can't buy live peanut bunker in most places along the east coast. Luckily, they're easily gathered with a cast net. Six-foot nets will do the trick early in the season when peanuts can be located in the shallows, but once the migration begins in earnest most of the baitfish will be found in eight to 20' of water. The six-foot cast nets become ineffective in water over four feet, and in these deeper areas, a 10' cast net with relatively wide mesh (so it sinks quickly) is necessary. A 12' net is better, but the larger the net, the tougher it is to throw. You can locate the baitfish with one of two methods: cast your net around piers and bridges with bright lights just before sunrise, or putt slowly along and look for the tell-tale flips of menhaden at the surface. Although it takes a little more effort to wake up and be on the water prior to sunrise, netting around lights is definitely the most effective way to gather these baits. Since the fish are concentrated, commonly it'll just take a cast or two to fill the well. Chasing them in open water after the sun is up, however, sometimes takes hours. At the very tail end of this migration, when just about all of the fish have moved deeper and will be tough to find, you may have the best luck by simply blind-casting around channel edges.

Once the livewell's full of peanuts, head for those channel edges and points and drift your baits across the bottom. If bluefish are still in town forego live-lining them on the surface, where they're most likely to shred the baits. But if the marauders have departed for the season you'll likely pick up additional stripers by letting a bait or two swim out freely near the surface. Remember to scale down the tackle according to the bait size. When the fish strikes a three-count will lead to more hook-ups than an immediate hook-set, but a five-count is too long and will produce gut-hooked fish.

One more specific live baiting technique that's worth examining is bunker snagging. During the summer and fall months in areas of relatively open water, you may spot isolated, small (the size of a boat or two,) schools of adult-sized menhaden swimming at or near the surface with no apparent predators attacking the baitfish. Quite often, however, these schools do have a large (30" or longer) bass or two shadowing it. You won't see the fish breaking water very often, because it's not so much actively hunting the school as it is just hanging close by, waiting for a weak or injured bunker to fall behind for a moment and make for easy pickings. Cast lure after lure through the school, jig around it, or troll past it, and you're probably not going to catch these rockfish. In fact, most of you have probably seen schools of bunker like this, fished around them for a while, and wondered where the heck the stripers were.

The way to get these fish to bite is to give them what they want: one of those menhaden, gone lame. To do so, you'll need a "bunker snagger," which is essentially a large treble hook with lead wrapped around the shank. You can make one yourself, by wrapping a pliable lead strip (cut an inch off one of those used for waterfowl decoy weights, for example) around the shank of a hook. In a pinch, tying a treble hook onto your line with a sinker tied on two or three feet below it will work, too. Cast it well beyond the school of bunker, give it a moment to sink, then rip it through the school quickly. After one or two shots, you should snag a bait.

These full-grown menhaden are much harder to keep alive than peanut bunker, and unless you have a large livewell with lots of flow, don't even try to catch more than one bait at a time. Simply pull off the bunker snagger and clip on a live-lining rig, with no additional weight. Run the hook through the fish's nostrils and then flip the menhaden back into the school. With a hook in its head the menhaden will struggle wildly to keep up with its school-mates, and it won't take long for that big striper to spot his easy meal. Note that you'll want to give them plenty of time to eat, as even a 30" or 40" fish will take a few seconds to suck a 10" menhaden all the way down.

Once this technique has been practiced successfully, it's usually time to move on. You may pick up a second striper from a school of bunker, but most of the time you'll find a loner or perhaps a pair in this situation but catching additional fish is rare.

Tactics
Eeling

Eels are most commonly drifted, although some anglers do slow-troll them. Eeling is usually done in the fall and winter months, when the fish have either schooled or are at least gathered into pods. In some areas eeling is illegal in the spring, since most stripers suck eels down with such vigor that they're often gut-hooked. One great perk to eeling: you won't catch many small fish. It's rare if not impossible to catch a striper under 24" on a foot-long eel, and more commonly, 30"-plus fish are the ones slurping them down.

Eeling is most effective when you can pinpoint the fish at a particular structural break, on a piling or series of pilings, or on a bump or series of bumps. Generally speaking, if the tide has the stripers in a feeding mood and you put a live eel in front of the fish, it'll eat. So wise eelers will stick with a spot if they're sure it holds fish, and work it through the tidal cycle even if they don't catch anything at first. At the rips in the North Carolina inlets during the winter, for example, you could often fish at one specific spot for five hours straight without ever having a bite. Then during that sixth hour, when the tide is correct in that exact same spot, you might catch a dozen 30" to 40" fish. So—what's the magic hour? As usual, it depends. It varies from season to season, and you'll have to spend some time to determine the pattern before you can put your foot down and say exactly when the fish will bite during any given season. (Usually once you do so, they'll change the pattern... of course.) Generally speaking, however, eeling is usually best right at the change of the tide. Quite often it's also hot at the peak of the current, which usually occurs an hour to a half hour before the change (depending on your location.)

This Delaware striper couldn't resist the wiggling eel. Note the cuts in the eel—there were bluefish in town, too.

Bonus Factoid
Eeling Tip

Dragging across the bottom you'll feel lots of "false" strikes as your weight bounces over shells, rocks, and the like, and that can make it tough to know whether to abandon a spot or give it another try. To determine if you're really getting hits, and should thus stick around for another drift or two, look for ring-shaped scratch marks around the eel. If they're visible it's a sure sign stripers have been trying to eat them. If not, chances are all you felt were false bites.

Once you've pin-pointed that fish-holding location, it's usually most effective to drift the eels over it as opposed to anchoring. The exceptions, as with other live bait fishing, occur when fish are orienting to a particular break in an inlet jetty, or when the wind or current is so strong it's impossible to drift fish.

Okay, you've got the spot? Pull up-current, position your boat so it will drift back over the fish, shift into neutral and lower away. Make sure you let out enough line to keep that eel right on bottom, and wait for the thumps. Thumps? Yes, thumps. Stripers take eels in a unique fashion. Usually when one hits you'll feel a series of fairly gentle thumps, three or four in a row, separated by a fraction of a second. Set the hook now, and you'll come up empty. Instead, start a five-count the moment you feel the first thump. By the time you reach five, the thumps should have ended and the striper should be pulling on the line consistently; it's choked the eel down and now it's swimming away. When you're confident the thumps have turned into tugs set the hook firmly, and the fight will be on.

If you feel two or three sharp, strong twangs on the line instead of the thumps, you'll need to reel up and check your bait. Usually, you'll pull in a half or a quarter of an eel, thanks to a bluefish. Rip it off and start over, because those stripers want an eel that's whole, live, and wiggling.

CHAPTER NINE

STRIPERS ON THE FLY
Where art and sport collide.

The popularity of fly fishing among striper anglers has soared in the past decade. Up and down the coast, inland and on the beach, for schoolies and for cows, there are huge numbers of dedicated fly anglers. Where and when is fly fishing for stripers at its best? In short, anywhere at any time the fishing is good for other types of angling with lures. It is most certainly at its easiest when fish are feeding at the surface. A proficient fly angler, however, can match and sometimes exceed the effectiveness of other forms of fishing on the surface, come close to matching it when fish are in relatively shallow water, and can still do pretty darn good when the fish are deep if he knows what he's doing. Note to readers: that proficient fly angler would not be me. It should be mentioned at this point that I am barely competent with a fly rod in my hands, and am no expert at fly fishing by any stretch. So, I had to depend on information provided by outside sources to write this chapter. Thanks go out to Pete McDonald, Rocky Calia, Jack Saum and Aden King. I'd also like to mention Lefty Kreh. I've only talked to him a few times in my life and he did not contribute to this book, short of serving as a role model for me when I decided to start writing about fishing. But if it weren't for the many books he's written on fly fishing, I never would have picked up a fly rod in the first place. If you really want to develop your talents at fooling rockfish with flies, get some of Lefty's books.

Tackle

The most important thing to remember about fly fishing gear is that you are not attempting to cast the lure, you are casting the line. Thus, your line/rod match is extremely important. Casting the line as opposed to the lure or bait has some advantages: you do not have to retrieve the lure all the way in, every time you wish to make a cast. You can make partial casts, such as a roll cast, to re-present

Dedicated fly angler Jack Saum fights a schoolie. Note the stripping basket, which keeps the stripped fly line contained in boats that aren't snag-free.

the lure in a specific area at a moment's notice. You can make minor adjustments in line length and accuracy by making false casts, without ever having to reel in and re-cast. And since flies can be custom-tied (by some experts, even on the spot) you have a better ability to match the hatch than you do in other forms of fishing.

Of course, there are trade-offs. Some disadvantages fly anglers face: Wind—a common factor in saltwater fishing—can make casting a fly difficult. In some situations, casting in some directions may be virtually impossible. Getting your offering to depths beyond a few feet can be difficult, especially when current is a factor. Getting it to depths beyond 25' or so may be essentially impossible at times. Fly casting requires a lot of room, and on a crowded boat you're as likely to hook a fellow angler (or a radio antenna, outrigger, T-top, etc.) as you are a fish. It requires multiple knots for most lure or rig changes; complete line changes to match conditions at times; more practice to master effectively than other types of fishing; a substantial equipment investment to get started; and is greatly enhanced by mission-specific boats which can cost a lot of money. After saying all that, let's not forget one more thing: it's a heck of a lot of fun, too.

Fly rods are rated by the size of the line they are designed to handle. In plain English, the higher the number is, the heavier the gear. Generally speaking, for schoolies you'll find a seven-weight rod provides lots of fun and enough beef to get the fish to the boat. Larger stripers require nine-weights, and if you have the opportunity to go after real trophies with fly gear, you can move all the way up to a 12-weight. Serious aficionados will even surf fish for stripers with fly gear this size.

A long rod of eight and a half feet or more will boost casting range and control, but will be harder to use in cramped quarters. For most saltwater boat anglers, an eight footer is about right for an all-around rod. Remember to go on the shorter side if you spend most of your fishing time on boats, and go longer if you intend to cast more from shore.

You can get a beginner's rod for as little as $100 but will soon outgrow it, and feel the desire for one of those zillion-dollar boron rigs. Most serious anglers trend this way, and it explains why most fly anglers have another item that the rest of us tend to ignore: a rigid rod case. If you're going to spend all those bucks on a nice rod, remember to provide it protection.

Single-action reels work fine for fly fishing, since you do the retrieving and applying drag with your fingers. Some anglers to like to get more advanced reels with which drag can be applied, but using them effectively is easier said than done. Since you'll often have many feet of stripped line sitting on the deck or in a basket when the strike comes, to retrieve with the reel and drag you'll first have to either let the fish swim out with the line you've already retrieved until it comes tight against the reel, or crank up the piled line with one hand while attempting to fight the fish at the same time, with the other hand. Since you also need a hand to hold the rod, this can be quite difficult for most two-handed mortals. Obviously, it takes a seasoned angler to become proficient at either of these tactics. These reels also weigh a lot more than single-action reels, and can affect your casting ability. When all is said and done, it's best for the majority of us to stick with single-action models, until we feel extremely competent or grow a third hand.

Fly line comes in many varieties and a different type is needed to match each fishing situation. Floating lines, obviously, can be used when the fish are at or near the surface. Sinking lines will be necessary when the fish are deeper. There are countless varieties of sinking and partially sinking lines, each designed to meet a different particular requirement. Fly lines with sinking forward sections, called sink-tips or shooting heads, are quite often of use to striper anglers since they allow better castability than full sinking lines yet still allow you to probe deep. These lines are, however, no picnic to cast; you'll have to throw out the sinking part (which varies in length) then strip out as much line as you hope to cast onto the deck or into a stripping basket. Once the line's out of the reel, you can start casting again to get the heavy section into the air. Get some momentum going, then "shoot" the line out, and its weight will carry out most or (hopefully) all of the line you have sitting on the deck or in your basket. A 30' sink tip, for example, can be used to carry out at least 50' to 70' of additional line, depending on how proficient a fly caster you are.

Many anglers purchase spare spools for their reels, and load them up with different lines so they're always ready to match the conditions they encounter. In fact, so many anglers consider line such an important part of their arsenal that entire product lines have been developed to target specific fish, including our own favorite. Scientific Anglers, for example, makes 17 sinking lines in the Mastery Striper Series, which are all designed to match specific striper fishing situations. Which one will you want to use? That question requires an entire book to answer properly. There are literally dozens of choices of lines that fully or partially sink, those that have different sections that act one way or another, and those that sink at different rates. Remember that current will require heavier lines to sink to the same depth that still water requires, and the heavier it gets, the tougher it will be to cast effectively. With many weighted lines, in fact, certain common casting techniques (such as the roll cast) will be impossible to perform. Again: we can only cover the basics here, so you should read Lefty to become truly knowledgeable on this subject. That said, here are some general rules of thumb: most of the time striper anglers working the shallows will use floating lines. Those fishing the upper to middle water column will want to use sink-tip lines, as opposed to sinking lines. These will get your fly down a few feet, but still allow you to cast well and visually keep track of the fly line. A 350-grain sink tip, which sinks relatively fast, is a good starting point. It allows you to probe below the surface effectively but by stripping the line back fairly quickly, you can also tempt fish that are sticking to structure in the eight to 15' foot depth range. And when you're trying to get to fish 15' or more beneath the surface, you'll need to switch to the full sinking lines.

So, that's it for fly lines, right? Wrong—you still have leaders to worry about. Except that fly guys don't like to call them leaders, they call them "tippets." And you may have guessed this already, but there are about ten zillion different types, to match each and every conceivable situation one could ever encounter on the water. Quite often, these are a combination of different pound-tests, or a taper-ing leader that goes from a heavy to a lighter test as it reaches the end. Tapered tippets such as these help you make better casts and presentations, as opposed to regular leaders. The taper allows the energy in your cast loop to flow down towards the fly, and turn it over so it lands straight out. This also helps prevent the fly from snagging on the leader as the loop travels down the tippet. Using a tapered leader you'll experience fewer wind-knots, fly line tangles, and casts that end with the fly dropping on top of the fly line.

Like they say on TV: but wait, there's more! You may also need a shock tippet in certain situations. Usually, these will be help-ful when fishing around docks, rockpiles, jetties, and other structure which can abrade the line. Shock tippets should be noticeably heavi-er than the main tippet, and in heavy, barnacle-covered structure, some anglers will go as high as 40 pound test. These are commonly very short sections of line, only a foot or two in length. Even so, they will make casting a bit tougher.

When fishing in bluefish-infested waters, many fly anglers will also use a trace of wire at the end of the tippet. Note: if you're in this boat, try using Tyger brand leaders. They can be tied in regular knots, are quite flexible, and are much easier to cast than traditional wire.

When it comes to lures, fly anglers are again faced with limit-less possibilities—even more so than the average spin or conven-tional angler, since the fly guy may well tie his own lures with unique color patterns or combinations. Most fly fishermen will be casting streamers, clousers, deceivers, and other flies which resemble bait-fish as they move through the water. As usual, stick to the old adage: if it ain't chartreuse, it ain't no use. However, red/white and purple/black are also effective color combinations, particularly in discolored water or low-light conditions. Often, fly anglers plying the waters for stripers will find that flash adds a lot of action. Tinsel, glitter strips, and holographic eyes all work together to improve the bite ratio, par-ticularly in bright conditions. Again, note that in low light or stained waters the flash will not necessarily help, and may be out-fished by dull, dark flies. And at times, lures with a mirror-like or metallic finish will go untouched—go figure. Anglers working in the shallows, particularly in mud flats, sod banks, and tidal tributary rivers, will also do well with crab or shrimp patterns. These can be tied at home, bought by mail order, or can be purchased in Florida where they're sold as permit flies, but may be tough to locate in the mid and northern ranges of our target species. Poppers will prove effective anywhere the fish are apt to bust the surface. Many serious striper anglers, however, note that thin profile poppers definitely seem to garner better results than short, fat ones. Remember, we're trying to imitate the baitfish striper eat, not frogs. In any case, when purchasing streamers and other fish-imitating flies be sure to confirm they are saltwater-grade before making the purchase. Quite often, low-grade steel and metals which are used for freshwater flies will deteriorate in a matter of hours after their first use in salty conditions.

Another factor that holds true with other types of striper fishing—you'll want to match the hatch. When stripers are busting through schools of tiny bay anchovies, two-inch thin-profile crystal minnow will do the trick. When they're popping schools of sand eels, use a sand eel pattern. Resin spoons, which are one of the few flies to provide their own action, are also effective in many schooled-bait situations. But when the fish are chasing larger bait go to flies with more bulk and larger profiles. Some nine-inch flies designed to imitate skipjack and bonito for marlin can be quite effective when big stripers are pouncing on full-grown menhaden. Of course, that's a dream more often than a reality. Commonly, a four-inch chartreuse clouser is probably one of the simplest, most effective starting points when you don't know exactly what the fish are after just yet.

Stripping baskets should also be mentioned, because they will be a necessity for some boat anglers. Generally speaking fly guys seem happier stripping their line directly onto the deck. But that requires a smooth, snag-free section of the boat. Unless you have a flats boat or a bay boat that's designed with fly fishing in mind, chances are you'll have cleats, running lights, rails, and hatch pulls to contend with. In this case, a stripping basket saves a lot of time and aggravation, by providing you with a snag-free spot to pile the line.

Tactics

When it comes to tactical applications in saltwater, the real difference between traditional fly fishing and fly fishing for stripers becomes crystal clear. Fishing tackle is fishing tackle and even when you're making the transition to saltwater, fly rods, reels, and even lures are essentially the same as freshwater stuff on steroids. Not so when it comes to tactics. Whether stalking brookies in a mountain stream, fishing for salmon in a river, or tempting tail-water trout, one casts the line out and allows the fly to drift naturally in the current. The fly is placed, and the bite awaited. Working the salt for stripers, however, requires an active retrieve. It's up to you to bring the streamer or popper to life, and you can't simply cast it out there, and watch.

Unlike spin and conventional casting gear, of course, you won't retrieve with the reel. Rather, you need to strip the line through the guides of your rod to give your offering motion. Treat the need to impart action as you would with any other type of fishing: when the water's warm and the fish are active, strip fast. When it's cool, keep things slower. One exception: the use of crab or shrimp-imitating flies combined with floating line will allow you to work your offering slowly in shallow waters, regardless of conditions. This can be quite effective when fish are holding tight to shoreline structure, such as sod banks, deadfall, stumps, rip-rap, or pier pilings.

You can strip line at essentially any rate you deem necessary to excite the fish. At times a twitch of the wrist, bringing in two or three inches of line, is all you'll want. At others, arm-length strips may be necessary. As a general rule remember that more and faster strips impart much more action, and a more erratic action, than fewer and longer strips. To vary the retrieve some fly anglers will add pauses between the strips, and/or change the length of each strip, as well as the speed.

When fishing any type of structure, focus on the same strike zones as you normally would. To place your fly at the depth the fish are feeding at you'll usually have to over-cast the target, give it a matter of seconds to sink, then strip at an appropriate rate of speed. Naturally, sink time and stripping rate will vary depending on the amount of current you have, and the type of line you're using. Considering the multitude of conditions one could encounter at a single bridge piling through one cycle of the tide, it quickly becomes apparent why so many serious fly anglers carry those different spools of line all the time!

As usual, there has to be an exception to the rule. In this case, it's with chum flies. Although some fly anglers consider it un-sporting, many will tie flies which look more or less like a bloody chunk of fish the size of your thumb nail, and drift it back in a chum slick. Despite the protests of some gentrified anglers, this tactic should be considered, especially by novices. It will give you the opportunity to hook and fight large numbers of fish on fly gear, and thus become proficient at hook-sets and fights on this type of equipment. In short, it's good practice.

Fishing a chum fly is simple. As with chum baits, you'll simply want to allow the fly to drift back in the slick with the other chum chunks, no additional action necessary. Sometimes fish will swim right up and grab a chum fly that's held in position behind the boat, and other times you'll have to drift it back naturally so it sinks with the other chum bits. As usual, a variety of lines must be on-hand to match the effective technique in order to maximize success. That said, this is probably about the easiest way to hook a striper on fly gear, and quite often, an easy to cast floating line is all that's needed.

Setting the hook is very different with fly gear than traditional gear, and is commonly misunderstood by novice fly anglers. While spin and conventional anglers retrieve with the rod tip at an angle, then jerk back to set the hook, savvy fly anglers retrieve with the rod tip pointed directly at the line and lure. Since he or she strips constantly, the line is always in the angler's hand. Obviously, since the bait is always an artificial, there's no wait-time before setting the hook. The moment a bite is detected, the angler jerks back with the hand holding the line to set the hook home, then lifts the rod tip up and out to apply tension and bring a bend into the rod. At this point, the fish can be fought with a combination of pressure from the bent rod and tension applied by the angler pulling (or releasing) the line. How do you judge how much tension to put on the line? Sorry, there's no magic bullet here. You just have to gain the "feel" for when the different tippets you use are going to break, and that only comes with experience. That said, if you want to gain as much experience as possible while losing as few fish as possible, try casting at a chain-link fence with a fly that has a large gap hook. (Use a fly you don't much care about, because it will get trashed.) When you hook the fence, slowly apply pressure until your tippet breaks. After a few hours of breaking off and re-tying, you'll start to get a feel for just how much oomph that particular tippet can take.

Remember—point the rod tip right at the fish, and set the hook with a solid yank. If you're fishing a sinking line and it leaves the tip-top at an angle to the fly, don't be afraid to stick the tip of your rod into the water to eliminate that angle. Keep the direct connection right until the moment the fish is solidly hooked. More stripers are probably lost on flies because of the angler's habitual motion of raising the rod tip upon the strike, than because of any other mistake. Trout have delicate mouths, and lifting the tip is all it takes to get a hook in there. Most anglers who fly fish learned while going for trout, and are conditioned to react accordingly. But if you try this tactic with stripers you'll miss fish after fish after fish as all the pressure you apply is absorbed by the bending rod tip.

One final note: when you go fly fishing in the salt, bring along an extra bottle of freshwater and a clean rag. You'll notice as the day progresses, it may become tougher and tougher to cast. Your line seems sluggish, and harder to lift. This is because salt will adhere to and dry on many fly lines. When your casts seem to lack their usual luster, pile all of your working line onto the deck. Soak the rag in the freshwater, then wrap it around your line where it comes out of the reel. Squeeze the rag gently as you reel the line through the wet rag, to remove the offending salt. Rotate or change the rag's position every few second so the salt doesn't pile up in one spot. Before re-casting, check your rod's line guides, which may also gather a salty coating, and clean them as necessary.

CHAPTER TEN

NIGHT FISHING

The most under-rated method of striper fishing on the planet—give this a try.

Ever notice how big a striper's eyes are? Compared to our eyes, when you consider body size and weight, they've got to be five times as big. Why? At least one reason is that stripers like to feed at night.

You can target rockfish in the dark at just about any time of the year, but perhaps the best time to do so is during the heat of summer. Through July and August, night fishing is often 10 times more effective than fishing during the daylight. High summer temperatures drive stripers deep during the day, and often you can see piles of them on the meter yet can't buy a bite. Those same fish will feed strongly once the sun goes down.

You can night fish for stripers anywhere you'd find them during daylight, with some degree of success. And you can also find rockfish prowling the shallows at night, when the bright sunlight encountered in shallow water during the day has gone away; those large eyes are a bit light-sensitive, and striped bass can get pushed down by the brightness. But the very best places to night fish for stripers aren't their daytime haunts nor the shallows. The spots that attract stripers the most are those with artificial lights.

Lights can be found around lighted bridges, piers, bulkheads, and ships. You can also set up your own artificial lights, right from your own boat. In all of these cases, the area where the artificial light peters out and darkness takes over is called the light-line—and light-lines are where the predators hunt.

Most anglers will fish pre-existing artificial lights when they go night fishing. These can be easily scouted out once dark has hit, or you may know of some simply from driving over bridges on your way to the boat ramp. But you should have a specific spot in mind to head for when you launch for an evening of night fishing, and plan to be there and be anchored up before the sun has sunk completely

Night time is often the right time, for big stripers.

behind the horizon. It's both safer and less stressful to be in position as opposed to running after dark, even though you will still have to run to get back home when you're done fishing.

Tackle

A statement of the ridiculously obvious: one piece of gear you'll need is a flashlight. But unlike other after-dark activities, you'll need both hands free to tie knots, bait hooks, and so on. So look for a hands-free light, like the clip-on Pelican lights ($15 at most outdoors or camping stores) which secure to a hat brim. Petzel and Survival Systems also make good hands-free versions but these are a bit more expensive and run between $30 and $50; they're available at REI or Bass Pro Shops. Red lights are better than white ones, because they don't ruin your night vision. White lights will make it impossible to see for minute or two once you turn them off, especially on white fiberglass boats which produce a ton of glare. And go for LED bulbs if you have the option, because they have an extremely low draw and your batteries will last a lot longer.

These lights to see by are important, but they're not the most important illumination onboard. That would be the fish-attracting night lights you got for your boat—and the more light you can put on the water the more bait you'll attract. The more bait you attract, naturally, the more big fish you'll catch. White halogens work well; for years I used a set attached to a broomstick, which I dropped into a rodholder and aimed at the water. But in recent years green fluorescent lights like the Hydro Glow ($200, www.meltontackle.com) and the Green Magnet ($150 - $190, www.baitlight.com) have been developed, and they are truly amazing. These two to four foot long tubes will throw a halo of green light 30' around the boat, and menhaden are attracted to it like moths to a porch light. In fact, I've watched schools of menhaden numbering in the thousands circle around them in a swarm so thick, they blocked the light until the green glow was a mere sliver. At times like these, one throw of the cast net provides a livewell full of prime baits and a swarm of predators is usually not far off.

Bonus Tip for Offshore Anglers	**Bonus Tip for Crab Lovers**
These lights are also just as effective at attracting squid and tinker mackerel in blue water.	*When you put one of these lights over the side also keep a dip net handy, because they attract crabs, too.*

Blue, pink, and several other color lights are also available, but in testing I did for an article in Boating Magazine we tried different colors in several different situations, and without fail the green lights attracted the most bait. Manufacturers claim that the blue lights are visible from farther away and thus draw fish in from greater distances. Maybe they're right, but in every situation I've been in, green is the killer.

Some anglers also use small lights or cylume light sticks that attach directly to their lines, usually at the line-to-leader swivel, as one would use when swordfishing in the Atlantic canyons. I'm not convinced that helps much, although this may be because their effect is dampened by the overwhelming light of a unit like the Hydro Glow. It should also be mentioned that there are knock-offs on the market. Bass Pro Shops has their own version of green night lights, as do a couple of other companies. While I'm sure they work I can't vouch for them, as I haven't tried them personally.

Another tool all night anglers need is a good handheld spotlight. You shouldn't cruise with it on, since it will destroy your night vision. But a strong spotlight is invaluable when you're trying to find channel markers and other landmarks in the dark. Remember, however, not to aim it at other boaters. This will only blind them.

With each of these types of lights, you'll be burning more than the usual amount of juice. After a few hours of night fishing it's quite common to have low or dead batteries, so you should always carry a spare 12-V power pack or a jumper pack onboard. In fact, it's best to carry an extra 12-V deep cycle battery dedicated to powering your night lights, alone. Remember to secure it well before running—a 12-V battery sliding across the deck can do some serious damage.

Some additional safety gear is in order when you go night fishing. Every angler should wear a life jacket, for starters. If you haven't seen the inflatable life belts, check them out. They're so lightweight and comfortable you forget they exist, and there's really no reason to argue against their use. Every angler should also be outfitted with a cyalume light stick and a thick rubber band. Use the rubber band to attach the light stick to a belt loop or the wrist, and activate the light stick at the beginning of the evening. That way, if anyone does happen to go overboard at least they'll be armed with a light source you can spot. Everyone should also have a sound-making device in a pocket or attached to their life vest; whistles work best for this purpose.

What kind of rigs should you use at night? Essentially, the same as you would during daylight, with a few caveats. First off note that at night, bait will usually out-fish lures by a wide margin. As usual you'll want to match the hatch, but in general live bunker or spot, cut peeler crab chunks, whole clams, and fresh menhaden chunks get top billing. Notice a trend? These are stinky baits, and that stink will help the stripers home in on your offering. That's not to say, however, that you can't use lures effectively at night. You can, with the best results occurring along light lines and with lures fished at or near the surface. Surface disturbers like poppers or prop-baits will draw in more fish than lures that don't create vibrations, and in inlets and around jetties with lots of current—where natural baits may well be lost in short order—artificials may even out-produce the real thing. If you're going to try artificials remember that three colors usually out-produce the others in the dark: purple, black and (of course) chartreuse.

Another exception to night versus daylight fishing similarity is the level of surface action. At night stripers will often prowl slightly below the surface, while looking in an upward direction. They do this because it's easier to see the silhouette of their prey while looking up from below, with either moonlight or artificial light back-lighting the baitfish. As a result if you have live baits you'll often do better by live-lining them with no weight whatsoever. Run your hook through their nose or jaws to encourage swimming near the surface, instead of hooking through the back, which encourages baitfish to swim downward. And if you are casting lures, use light ones or floaters which you can work at or near the surface. With cut baits, drifting them down through the light-lines with no added weight is another good bet.

So far as rods and reels go, all bets are off. You may want to night fish with 10-lb. spinning gear, or you may want to use 40-lb. conventional gear, and either can be as effective as the other. Generally speaking, however, it's safe to up-size leaders a bit when night fishing. In the dark, even 50- or 60-lb. test seems to go unnoticed.

Tactics

As usual, when fishing at night you'll want to position your boat where the fish are. Not as usual, that means looking for and hunting at light lines. And it also means fishing from an anchored boat is almost always better than fishing from a moving boat. The fish are orienting to a particular situation and/or structure, so you'll want to stick with it. Your lights will draw fish in, and stick with you in that one spot. Also, remember that it's night time—navigating is much more dangerous than it is during daylight, and requires 100-percent of the captain's attention. Try fishing while adrift at night and unless you're foolhardy, you simply won't be able to relax and fish.

Consider that the rockfish are going to be ambushing baitfish that they can see in silhouette, by darting up from below. Naturally, the striper doesn't want to be spotted before he initiates the attack. So they'll often prowl along the dark side of the light line, and attack right where the light fades into darkness. To take advantage of this fact, you'll want to position your boat either in the dark side or in the light, then cast towards the light-line where the two meet. Wait a sec—why even worry about it, if you have these supposedly awesome night lights hanging off the boat? Two reasons: first, once you have the boat more or less in position you can fire up your lights, and see how far the light-line they create is from the light-line you

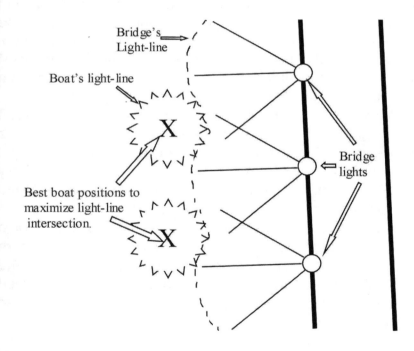

Set up near an artificial light line, then fire up your own lights. Then, adjust your boat's position so the two light-lines meet in as large an area as possible, and you'll be creating a spot that's twice as hot as it was when the sun went down.

have set up next to. Then you can re-adjust your position so that the two light-lines intersect—and now you've just created a doubly-good light-line. Second, having both your own lights and a pre-existing light-line allows you to fish multiple lines over multiple areas of light and dark, instead of clustering them along a single light-line.

It's worth stressing again that you should concentrate your efforts high in the water column at night. Keep retrieves up near the surface and don't shy away from a quick retrieve, if that's what it takes to keep that lure up top. Suspending bait from bobbers will work sometimes, but it's not a natural presentation and usually is not the prime method of catching fish. Slightly more natural looking is getting the bait itself neutrally buoyant or nearly so, which can be accomplished by cutting a chunk of foam off of a swimming noodle or packing peanut, and stuffing it into the bait. This tactic works best with peeler crab, since you can often find a spot in the shell to jam the foam into (try the "knuckles," or the corner of the back shell).

Another excellent way to present a stinky (read: delicious) bait to stripers at night is to fish it on a bucktail. A quarter or half ounce head is light enough that you can keep it up near the surface, yet you can find ones with long hooks and hair, that present a relatively large profile. Add a chunk of peeler crab or a strip of menhaden to the hook, and you'll have a doubly-attractive bait.

Since the fish are drawn in by scents as well as lights, you'd think chumming at night would be a good move. And it is—if there aren't any bluefish around. But if there are blues within 100 miles and you set out both lights and chum, you'll probably end up swarmed with snappers. They often move in and feed so hard, you can't even get a bait down to the stripers.

Bonus Night Fishing Tip

In many areas that you find stripers, there will also be weakfish present for at least part of the season. If this is true where you night fish, take note of the fact that the tactics and gear described in this chapter will bring weakfish to your boat as well, often in droves. The one difference: they'll be hanging out either at or near the underwater light-line where the artificial light from above peters out, or they'll be on bottom. Just how deep the underwater light-line is will depend on the water clarity and turbidity where you fish, but usually will be somewhere between 8' and 15' below your lights.

CHAPTER ELEVEN

RUDOW'S 10 FAVORITE STRIPER HOTSPOTS

All unique in their own way, these are super-cool fishing spots.

There are two kinds of hotspots: those that offer a reliable "maybe" season after season, and those that pop up at one time or another and are red-hot for a single season or portion of a season. The reliable yearly hotspots may hold fish for five seasons in a row, or they may go blank for five in a row. But everybody knows about them and sooner or later, the fish usually reappear there. The pop-ups could happen anywhere at any time, and may not hold fish again for decades. Of course, there are spots that vary in-between one extreme and the other.

A lot of buddies give me grief for giving away all our good hotspots in how-to fishing articles. But I do so happily, without a moment's regret. Does a good spot get swarmed after an article runs in The Fisherman or another publication, or appears online? Occasionally. But what most people fail to realize is that all degrees of hotspots come and go. From one season to the next, you'll always have to keep searching out new places if you want to out-fish the rest of the guys in the marina. You can't simply return to old faithful year after year and expect to catch fish every time.

Two examples that prove the point: The Hill, at the mouth of Eastern Bay, offered red-hot chumming during the fall months in the late 90's and early 00's. Everyone knew about it, and there were literally hundreds of boats crammed onto the spot on weekend days. Once your chum line was established it was common to catch dozens of fish on each tidal cycle, with hits coming minutes after you set your first bait. Most were small, but they ranged in size all the way up to the occasional 35" or 36" fish. Yet after about 2002 the Hill more or less went barren. Few anglers fished there, and even fewer caught fish there. But just about everyone who owns a fishboat in the middle

Chesapeake Bay knows where the Hill is, and the first time there's a published report hailing the fishing here, it's likely to become a mad-house again. Sooner or later it will happen; you can bank on it.

Contrast this spot to the Mollie Spot, in the South River. The Mollie spot is an edge of an oyster bar about a mile south of the Rt. 2 bridge. The drop isn't awesome, and no one ever fishes here—it's not really a "known" hot-spot. (Though it is described in Rudow's Guide to Fishing the Chesapeake.) Yet in the early fall of 2001, my three year old daughter Mollie pointed to the water's surface as we drove along and said "let's fish here, Daddy." For no reason other than to humor her, I pulled back the throttle and took a cast. Yup, you guessed it—I caught a fish. So I took another cast. Then another. Long story short: The Mollie Spot was red-hot for the next month, and we enjoyed limit catches there on many trips. But the next season, there wasn't a fish to be found here. Nor the next after that, and I haven't caught a fish here since, despite checking it out a couple times every season. Will the fish ever re-appear here? Sooner or later in all probability, but who knows? But the Mollie Spot will never get the notoriety of The Hill. And thank goodness. This kind of spot—the unlikely place you found by accident or by prospecting or through plain dumb luck—is the best kind. It's the one that, when it's in gear, gets you a limit while nine out of ten anglers are going to the Hill and catching half-limits. It's the one that helps you out-fish the competition. Will I give these types of hotspots away? In a heartbeat. Because in the vast majority of the cases, there's plenty of time to enjoy the spot before word re-ally gets out about the one season wonder. And next season, it prob-ably won't produce. People will forget about it, and go right back to their old reliables, like the Hill. Three, five, or maybe even ten years later, when I'm cruising past, I'll stop to take a cast and discover that the fish have come back to that spot. And I'll enjoy it again... until word gets out.

Why give such info away in the first place? Reason number one: it's my job. That's part of what writing good how-to/where-to fishing articles is all about. Reason number two: what comes around goes around. If you let other people in on your hotspots, they'll tell you when they discover a new one. If you want to build up a reliable network that brings you the best fishing information possible, sharing your own secrets is the best way to get started. (So if this book helps you catch more fish, don't forget to shoot me an e-mail at lr@gearedupublications.com, to let me in on the hot bite you just found!)

That said, all of these top 10 hotspots are ones I've found extraordinary for one reason or another. Most are more or less "known" spots, with good all-around reliability. Though they may or may not hold fish today, it's a reasonable bet that at some point through the next season or two, they will.

1. The Love Point Mud Flats in the Upper Chesapeake

The Love Point mud flats, ranging from 30' to 50' near the LP buoy in the upper Chesapeake Bay, is an unusual area because it's the top spot around for catching early season big migrating spring cow stripers on light tackle. In most other areas you'll have to pull large, heavy trolling gear to catch these fish, but chumming while fishing large chunk baits set on bottom—the spring chumming method described back in chapter 7—works at its best on the mud flats. Remember, trollers will often catch higher numbers of fish, but that's on those broom-stick rods. If you want to fight a 35" to 45" fish on 10- or 12-pound test, come to the Love Point Mud Flats during the first couple weeks of the Chesapeake Bay trophy season in mid to late April.

Unfortunately, weather plays a huge role in this fishery and the quality of the fishing will vary quite a bit from season to season. Ideally, you'll want a spring with very little rainfall, and water temperatures in the mid to upper 40's. If it rains heavily the water will likely be muddied, and when the temperatures climb the fish seem more focused on migrating than on feeding—the stripers you'll catch here using the spring chumming methods are almost entirely post-spawn, and warm weather keeps them on the move.

Many people will be surprised at this choice since it's not far at all from the Susquehanna flats, which receives a lot more fanfare. And truth be told, light tackle fishing on the flats can be even more fun because you can hook into the big ones while casting jigs, bucktails and topwater plugs. But this area offers catch-and-release fishing only. Personally, I don't like to catch and release large numbers of spawning stock fish. Some are sure to be injured and/or die, which is a tremendous waste, and I'd rather take my one fish per day and leave the rest of them alone. For the record: I wouldn't ever dream of forcing this attitude on anyone else and feel that everyone out there should fish the flats once or twice for the experience. I've been there and done that, and see no need to hit those fish year after year. Plus, I like eating rockfish!

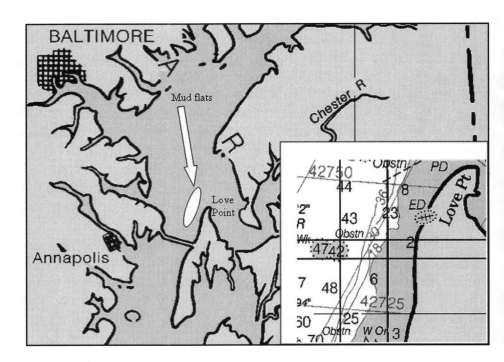

2. Hatteras Inlet, North Carolina

This place stands head and shoulders above most, because here, you can reliably catch huge stripers in the dead of winter. Again, part of the draw is that this is a light-tackle fishery. Eeling in the inlets is the name of the game which means spinning or conventional gear in the 12- to 17-pound range is on-target. While much of the rest of the coast is locked down in winter mode, Hatteras is downright hot.

If you want to go after these fish, remember that tides play a huge role. Don't even bother fishing unless you're within an hour and a half of the change of the tide. Cast your live eel up into the white water rips along the edges of the inlet channel, and wait for the take.

Small boats can get in on this action, since the fish are usually caught right where the calm inlet waters meet the rough stuff. During an outgoing tide, it's possible to anchor in completely calm water and let your eels drift back into roiled, fish-rich water. One should note, however, that there are shoals all over the place and if one is unfa-

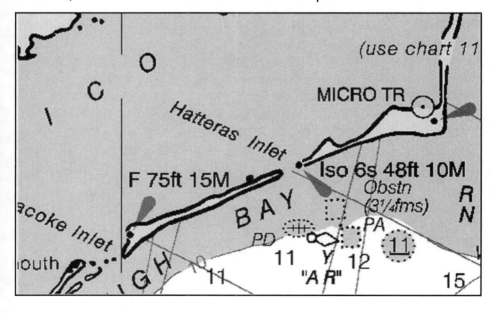

miliar with the inlet it's all too easy to run aground in it or on your way to it. Your best move is to either go with a local your first time out, or follow other boats and shadow them as they get into position.

If the weather allows (often it won't, during the winter months) and you have a larger boat at your disposal, spend the rest of your day trolling just outside of the inlet. Usually within a mile or two of the beach, there will large numbers of stripers on the prowl. While they won't hit the eels in the inlet on off-tidal cycles, they will often strike at umbrellas rigged with shad body teasers and parachute or bucktail hook baits, Stretch 30's, and tandem rigs.

3. Off the Gay Head Cliffs, Martha's Vineyard

Martha's Vinyard is an awesome place in the late spring, because you can tie into some truly massive rockfish here. The trick is to have good timing; arrive too early and you won't find the big fish, and arrive too late you'll spend all your time fighting bluefish. Mid May to early June is the time frame, but the exact timing of the best fishing will change from season to season and you have to keep one eye on the current reports, to get in on the big fish. Live herring are the best baits, and fishing them allows you to use light tackle. Unfortunately, they are also very hard to come by. Luckily, jigging and fishing cut bait will also tempt the big cows into biting.

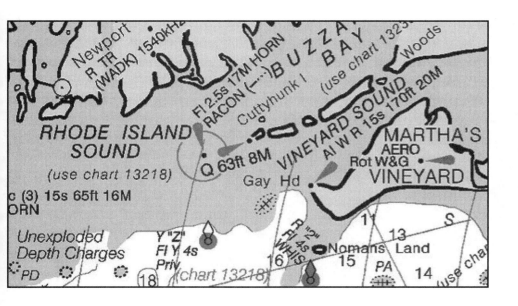

Try drifting along the rocky bottom just off of the cliffs at Gay Head, and along the drops and edges near by. You can also troll these areas (which is the usual course of business for many folks who can't come up with livies) and come up with some magnificent catches, though the use of heavy gear is required.

Late in the evenings, early in the mornings, and during periods of very low light you may also want to try surf casting from the island. Throwing popping plugs can produce savage strikes, when these fish move into relatively shallow water. At times, whole live bloodworms will also produce big fish in this surf.

4. The CBBT

The Chesapeake Bay Bridge Tunnel is like one massive fish reef. It stretches on and on for miles, has parts that run under the water's surface, and parts suspended over it. It has rockpiles, islands, pilings, and even wrecks in close proximity. And it has fish—lots of fish.

Casting under working birds, jigging over rockpiles, wreckage, and other bridge structure, and trolling all will produce catches that seem almost unreal at times. The fish can get extremely active here as early as October and go on a feeding binge that lasts into mid or

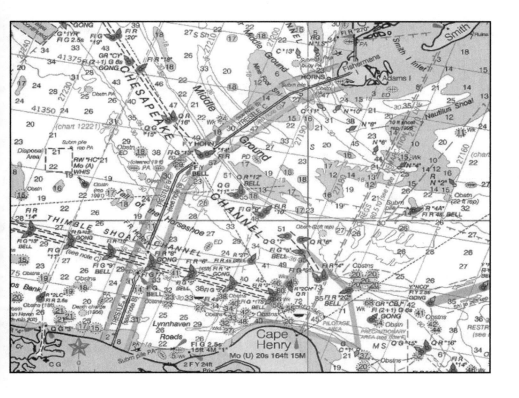

even late December. Flocks of working birds stretching out for acres, with stripers churning the water's surface below, are common. Large, medium and schoolie fish will all be available and willing to feed. Most seasons the average fish will be school sized but during the late fall or early winter the really big stripers move in about the time you expect the first snow. They don't orient to the bridge itself quite as much as the school-size fish do, and are usually taken by trolling as opposed to jigging or casting. But what really sets the CBBT apart from other areas to me is the fact that more often than elsewhere, really big fish can be found busting bait on the surface. Look for the birds, and you'll find 'em.

5. South Jersey's Sod Banks

The winding cuts and river-like channels going through the south Jersey shore present striper anglers with loads of light tackle opportunities. Fall is the time to bang the banks with bucktails, plastic jigs, or even topwater lures.

The fish here usually aren't monstrous and many of the areas near the ocean are inundated with snapper blues. They'll chew off your tails, eat the tail off your bucktail, and be a general pain in the butt to striper anglers. So, what's so cool about the sod banks?

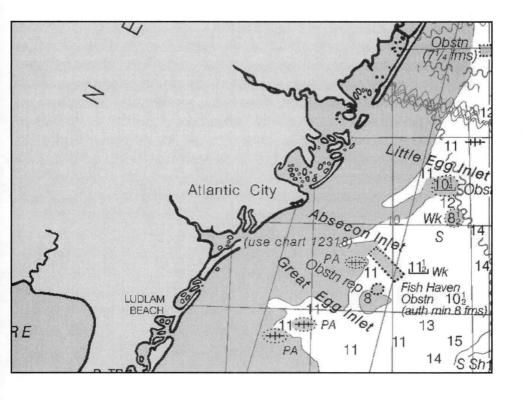

These areas can be fished with a small boat, in just about any conditions. The wind's blowing 20-knots and all you have is a 15' jon boat? No problem—go behind Brigantine or Avalon, and you'll have literally miles and miles of protected water that offers a good shot at hooking up and a reasonable shot at catching big fish. And, this is all light-tackle fishing. Casting with spinning, conventional or even fly gear is all appropriate, and will get some stripes on the end of your line. As an added plus, during the warm months of the year there are usually plenty of fluke in these cuts, as well.

6. Eastern Bay, in the Middle Chesapeake

During the fall season the rockfish in Eastern Bay will usually be schoolies in the 14" to 24" range, and they don't often go beyond the 32" to 36" range, (you'll find bigger ones early in the spring, but catching them here is prohibited.) But the sheer numbers are massive. At times, catching fish by the hundreds is not extraordinary.

They may be schooled up at the Hill, where currents swirl around a 24' to 50'-plus contour. Here, chumming is the name of the game. You may catch them up top or on the bottom, and they may

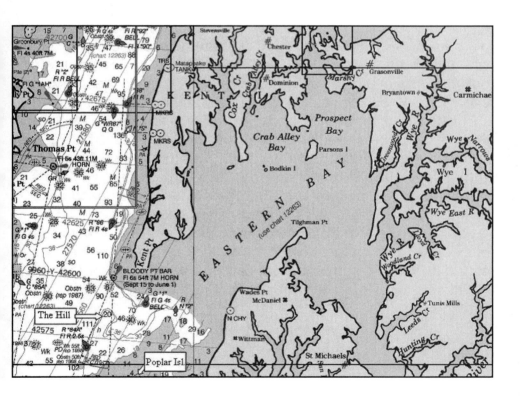

move in so thick that you can watch them eat the fish bits before they drift five feet from the boat. There's also a wide window of opportunity in Eastern Bay, opening up as early as late May and continuing through November. It's hit or miss—either they'll be there or they won't—but when it's a hit at the Hill, there's a good chance it'll be a home run.

Another hot Eastern Bay zone is the rip-rap surrounding the Poplar Island dredge containment facility. Here you'll want to toss four-inch twister tails, Bass Assassins, jerk baits, or shad body lures as close as possible to the rocks. Again, the fish could move in as early as May and could appear or hold here through the end of the season. Watch out for the sub-surface rockpiles off the sides of the rip-rap walls, which are completely covered at high tide. Smart anglers will make their first few trips here during a low tide, to figure out where it's safe to go and where it's not. Otherwise you'll risk wiping out your prop and/or lower unit. Get your jigs close to the rocks, however, and sometimes you'll get a strike on every cast.

Quite often in Eastern Bay, particularly from September through late November or early December, you'll find the rockfish tearing through schools of bay anchovies on the surface. These schools are usually relatively small, somewhere between the size of a large house and an acre, but there could be a dozen or more of them scattered across the area. They could pop up just about anywhere in Eastern Bay, and cruising around with a powerful set of binoculars while on the lookout for working birds is a recipe for success. No, you shouldn't expect to catch a new world record fish here. But there's a good chance to catch record-breaking numbers.

7. Fenwick Shoals

Six miles off the Delaware coast, Fenwick Shoals rise up to 20' or so from 45'. When the stripers are well into their fall migration, anywhere from mid November through December, depending on the weather, they'll hesitate here to feed. Most of the time eeling is the prime way to take these fish but quite often they'll be up top churning the surface, and you can catch them by casting plugs and surface chuggers. And these fish are big—running from 30" to 40" and larger—which makes this fishery extraordinary.

Like the Hatteras fishery it's tough to enjoy some seasons

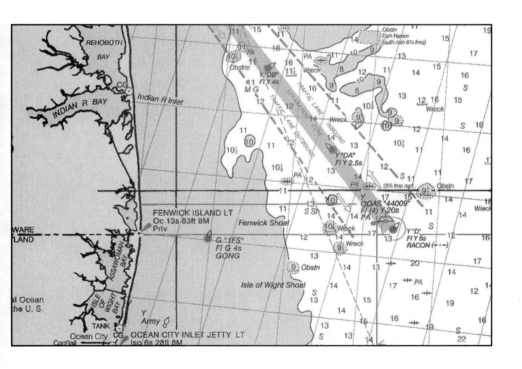

simply because the weather doesn't provide you with a decent window to go fishing. Especially for small boat anglers, you really have to pick the right day. Although it's only a few miles off the beach, the water at Fenwick Shoals can be extraordinarily rough, especially when 20-knot winds blow day after day.

When you can get out there and the fish are in town, this is another situation in which you'll want to bring a good pair of binoculars. Slowly cruise back and forth across the shoal—many anglers will pull a couple of lines as they do so—and keep a sharp lookout for those breaking fish. But remember—Fenwick Shoal is outside the three-mile federal waters limit, so (as of the time of this writing) you can't keep the stripers you catch here.

8. Manhattan, New York

Yes, you read that correctly—Manhattan. It would be more accurate to say the Hudson, but the towering New York skyline really is the main attraction here. For some reason, there's a unique draw to fishing right smack dab in the middle of the biggest city in the country. And believe it or not, the striper fishing around here is pretty darn good!

After centuries of development, decay, and redevelopment, there are broken down pier pilings, bulkheads, and marinas all over the place. Try casting jigs and Rat-L-Traps up near the detritus, and hold on tight. The Hudson has a healthy spawning stock of its own so the season is long, and fish can be caught around here just about

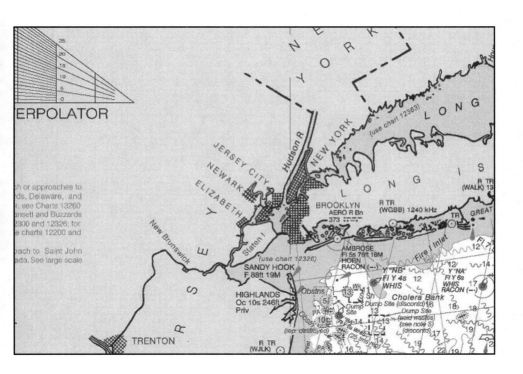

any time of year except for the dead of winter and very early in the spring, when the stripers head up-river to spawn.

If you're looking for a unique fishing experience, this is it. If you want to wow the kids with some one-of-a-kind city fishing action, here's the ticket. If you want to be able to claim you've caught stripers in the shadow of the Statue of Liberty, your time has come.

9. Cape May Rips/Mouth of the Delaware Bay

October is an awesome fishing month, up and down the coast. But if you had to pick one spot to hit after the leaves had changed color and started falling, it may well be the rips at the mouth of the Delaware Bay.

Overfall shoals, the Cape May Rips, and the surrounding shoals and contours are excellent places to get in your licks on 30"-plus size fish. These fish are headed south for the winter, and they're in full-blown feeding mode. The water is relatively shallow, so you can fish relatively light gear. Eeling, fishing live spot, and chunking with menhaden chunks are all favorite methods.

So, what sets this area apart from the others? The radically changing bottom combined with strong Delaware Bay currents combined with strong ocean currents often turn these waters into a washing machine—and there's something really cool about nailing big fish as you get thrashed by four-foot waves. It's man versus nature, man versus the sea, and apex predator versus apex predator, all rolled into one. I know this isn't everyone's cup of tea, but I think it's a hell of a charge—and some of you will, too.

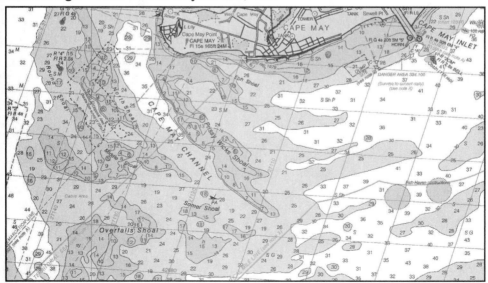

10. Lake Anna, Virginia

For those of us who grew up gunkholing around in salt water, there's something really bizarre about catching a striper in a lake. But it's another one of those experiences which every dedicated striper angler should have. You may find it a real challenge; tactics, lures, and tackle are quite different from what you may be used to.

Trolling is usually the best way to take these fish, but it's got to be in stealth mode. An electric trolling motor is the way to go, and side planers are used by savvy lake anglers to get their lures far away from the path of the boat. Diving plugs, Sassy Shads, Rat-L-Traps (my favorite in this situation) and spoons will all draw strikes, and the stripers you'll find in Lake Anna can be surprisingly large; 30" fish are not at all uncommon. For those who think they've done it all when it comes to striper fishing, this hotspot can provide new challenges and new frontiers...as well as dinner.

CHAPTER TWELVE

PROPER CATCH & RELEASE TECHNIQUES

Even more important than keeping your hooks sharp.

Okay, I know it sucks to sound preachy. But we have a problem here, you and I and all the rest of us who like to catch fish: there are zillions more people hooking stripers, and less and less stripers to hook. It is absolutely imperative that each and every angler out there know the proper release techniques to do as little damage to each fish as possible, when it's going to be let go.

Rule Number One: If you're catching throw-back after throw-back, go somewhere else. Even if you're a conservation deity with training from the CCA, DNR, and Wood's Hole Institute, you'll still kill a few fish here and there while catch and releasing them. You already know this is true—most of us just don't like to admit it. Reel up 20 or 30 little fish and regardless of what type of hook you use or how careful you are, one or two of them are going to get damaged. Maybe it'll be a gut squeeze, maybe a deep hook, maybe some slime removal or maybe a touched gill. Whatever. Face facts, and react to them—when you're catching throw-back after throw-back, it's time to move on.

Rule Number Two: If you're going to use baited circle hooks, make sure you have non-offset hooks. Everyone makes a huge deal about using circle hooks and frankly, it makes me sick—over 80-percent of the circle hooks on the tackle shop shelves are offset. Offset circle hooks will gut-hook fish just like J-hooks will. In the majority of the cases, the "circle" part is merely marketing hype on the part of the tackle manufacturer. In fact, these days you can find semi-circles that are barely curved at the point, and the package will be marked "Circle Hook." I hate to break the bubbles of many well-intentioned anglers, but much of this fuss is a gimmick and we have to be careful not to fall for it.

Exactly what is offset versus non-offset? Offset hooks have a bend which places the hook point and the shank of the hook on differing planes. Non-offset hooks have parallel shanks and points. Lay a hook on a table; if the point and shank both lie perfectly flat, it's non-offset. In most cases, this type of hook will set in the jaw as opposed to the gut. But if the point curves up off the table, it's an off-set—don't let it fool you.

If you really give a damn about taking advantage of the low-mortality offered by some types of tackle, you'll need to look carefully at every hook in your box. When you buy more hooks, you'll need to know exactly what works, and what doesn't. And if you're using off-set circles, remember that the mortality advantages gained by them are minimal, if any exist at all. When you buy, look for hooks that are explicitly marked "non-offset".

If you plan on harvesting the catch and are therefore using J hooks, you'll still need to be careful because catching undersized fish some of the time is impossible to avoid. You'll note that through-out this book, it's mentioned to give a three-count, or a five-count, and the following sentence mentions that longer counts result in a gut-hooked fish. It's up to you to use common sense when deciding how long to let a fish eat a bait. If, for example, you're catching a five-to-one ratio of throw-backs to keepers, don't give those fish the full five-count; cut it back a second or two. If you're jigging with a lure that has treble hooks, consider swapping out the treble for a single. (Note: this actually has much less of an effect than one would think, and your strike-to-hookup ratio won't go down very much at all.)

Rule Number Three: Touch the fish as little as possible. Keep-ing them in the water and using a de-hooker is about the best release method possible. You can buy de-hookers in most tackle shops, and you can also make one with a coat hanger, or other heavy pliable wire. The process is pretty simple: Bend a "u" shape into one end, then bend the other end into a square. Spin a bunch of duct tape around the square section to turn it into a handle, and you're good to go. This type of de-hooker only works properly when the fish are cleanly hooked, however. If the hook is buried down the fish's throat, you'll have to go to needle-nose pliers. What if the fish swallowed the hook clear down its stomach? Cut the line off as close to the fish as possible, and put it back over the side. Although it seems incredible that a fish can make it through the night with a hook in its gut, the scientists tell us that they can often survive the encounter.

"Lipping" the striper (inserting your thumb into its mouth and gripping the lower jaw between your thumb and forefinger) is the next best way to control the fish, while you remove the hook. If you can do it with the fish in the water, so much the better. If you have to handle the fish, dip your hands in the water first. Dry hands will remove the slime from the fish, and that slime is what protects the striper from disease and parasites—it's just like the fish's immune system. In fact, every few years I see a fish or two with mold-like

Wrap duct tape.

To build a de-hooker bend a square into one end of the wire, and a "U" in the other. Wrap the square in duct tape to turn it into a handle.

To release fish, place the "U" over your line and slide it towards the hook, while lifting on the de-hooker and pulling down on the line.

A home-made de-hooker takes moments to build and will help release fish without injury.

growth on its back, and can recognize the shape of a hand print. The worst thing you can possibly do is grip the fish with a dry towel. That's guaranteed to remove a huge amount of the slime and seriously harm the fish. Wet towels aren't so hard on the fish, but they don't really make it easier to grab the fish anyway. One caveat: feisty stripers will calm down and stop thrashing if you cover their eyes with a wet towel. If you have a large, hard to handle fish that you want to photograph or keep out of the water for a moment or two use this trick to keep it from thrashing around and injuring itself.

Bonus Pain-Saving Tip

If you fish around working birds and breaking fish, you've probably boated a gull or two by accident. This same towel-over-the-eyes trick works on seabirds, too. Toss a towel or T-shirt over a gull's head before you try to de-hook or untangle it, and you'll save yourself from a painful pecking.

Holding large fish up for a picture can hurt them, too. The fish's internal organs are not usually subjected to gravity as we know it, since the fish is supported by the water. Hefting one up out of the water can be enough to rip the fish apart inside. If you want to photograph the fish, lip it with one hand and support the fish's aft end with your other hand. Try not to grab or squeeze the fish around the belly, and remember that you'll minimize damage to the fish by minimizing the amount of time it's out of the water. Boga grips do a great job of controlling the fish while allowing you to keep it wet, and should be considered an imperative piece of gear for all serious catch and release anglers.

Another thing you should try to minimize, when releasing fish: fight time. The longer they struggle the more tired they'll be, making them less likely to survive release and more vulnerable to predators. So when you have a little fish on don't "play" it for long, and if you plan to catch and release up-size your gear before you make the first

A Boga grip will help you control the fish, without injuring it.

cast.

Rule Number Four: Never, ever, put your hand inside the fish's gill plate to hold it up. A fish's gills are its lungs. How would you like it if someone stuck their finger in your lungs? Doesn't sound too healthy, does it? Yet time and time again you'll see pictures of cow stripers with a guy's hand in its gills. Usually the caption reads something like "this big spawner was released after taking the photograph." Great idea, awful execution.

Rule Number Five: If you're netting the fish, use a shallow depth rubber-coated landing net. Knots and frayed ends scrape the fish and remove its slime, while the smooth rubber ones do a much better job of protecting the fish and are no less effective. In fact, you'll discover they also are easier to use because hooks don't tend to get snarled in the mesh, as often happens with nylon nets. While we're on the subject of nets: few people seem to know how to use them properly. Many anglers try to net stripers tail-first, which gives the fish a chance to swim away from the net. Others place the net into the water and have the fish swim into it, but I guarantee you the fish will avoid doing so if it is at all capable. The best way to net a fish is to hold the net out of the water until the fish's head is at or about to break the surface. Then dip and quickly scoop the net under the fish HEAD-FIRST, and raise it out of the water.

Rule Number Six: When considering how and where to go fishing, or whether or not to catch and release your fish, bear in mind that as temperatures rise and salinity drops, mortality goes up. In cool, salty waters the stripers have a much better chance of surviving an encounter with you and your fishing rod. But in warm, low-salinity waters, there's a good chance the fish won't make it. So reconsider before you decide to cast for mostly undersized fish with light gear way up-river in mid-August, because chances are most of the fish you throw back will end up belly up.

Rule Number Seven: Don't throw fish. It should bother you when you see people throw fish through the air, instead of releasing them gently. If a fish flies through the air then smacks down side-to, it may be injured from the impact and occasionally you'll see them go

Always net the fish head first!

into shock right after hitting the water.

Remember, the best way to release the fish is to de-hook it without ever handling it, and if possible, without ever removing it from the water. Of course, sometimes this simply isn't possible. To properly release the fish after boating it, support the fish's forward end by lipping it and the aft end by grabbing it just forward of the tail. Hold it at a 45-degree head-down angle to the water, and gently push it forward so it lands head-first into the water. This will give it a mouthful of water and force some water over the gills, so the fish gets a jolt of oxygen upon re-entry into the water.

Finally, we're at Rule Number Eight. (Whew!) If a fish isn't looking so good, don't give up on it right way. Pumping water through its gills will help revive the fish, and you can in effect force-feed it oxygen. The best way to do this is to hold the fish in the water by the lower jaw. If you're on a boat, put it into gear and move forward at minimal speed. Water will be forced into the fish's mouth and over its gills, feeding it a supply of oxygen. If you are on land and thus obviously can't move the fish forward through the water for minutes at a time, push it back and forth in such a way that as much water as possible is forced into the fish's open mouth. In either case, you'll know you've done your job well when you feel the fish attempt to bite down on your thumb. That's a sure sign of recovery, and tells you the fish is strong enough to attempt to swim again. As soon as it does so, remove your thumb from its mouth and give it a strong shove forward, away from shore, from the tail end.

Chapter 12

The Final Stripe

I sincerely hope you've enjoyed—and picked up a pointer or two—from Rudow's Guide to Rockfish. Die-hard anglers are always welcome to e-mail me questions, corrections, comments or (especially) up to date fishing reports at lr@geareduppublications.com.

Rudow's Guide To

FISHING THE MID ATLANTIC

38 Charts with More Than **300** Hot Spots!

COASTAL BAYS & OCEAN

BY LENNY RUDOW

If you're into fishing along the Atlantic coast you might want to check out Rudow's Guide to Fishing the Mid Atlantic, a how-to/where-to book which includes over 300 hotspots detailed on 38 custom-marked charts, covering from North Carolina to New York. The book includes sections on coastal bay, inlet, inshore and offshore fishing, tackle and tactics, and covers each specific species of fish found in the region, from sea bass to swordfish.

IT'S AVAILABLE AT WWW.GETGUP.COM

RUDOW'S GUIDE TO

Fishing

the

Chesapeake

Lenny Rudow

Inveterate Chesapeake Bay anglers should be interested in Rudow's Guide to Fishing the Chesapeake, which examines every tributary and main-stem area of the bay from its headwaters to the CBBT in detail. Hotspots are meticulously detailed on custom-marked charts, and separate sections of the book cover bay-appropriate tackle and tactics.

IT'S AVAILABLE AT WWW.GETGUP.COM

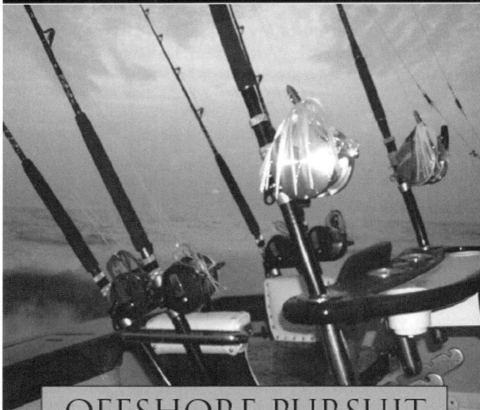

"John Unkart introduced me to a trolling rig I had never seen before, and the first day I tried it we hooked up with six bluefin tuna!" — Lenny Rudow, Boating Magazine's Ultimate Angler

OFFSHORE PURSUIT

BILLFISH · TUNA · WAHOO · MAHI-MAHI

OFFSHORE RIGGING AND TACTICS BY A PROFESSIONAL WITH 40 YEARS OF EXPERIENCE

BY JOHN UNKART

Hard-core offshore enthusiasts need to take a peek at Offshore Pursuit, by John Unkart, a professional mate with over 40 years of blue-water experience. From rigging techniques to tips on how to fight trophy fish, everything you need to know to hunt pelagics is covered in this book. Best of all, Unkart's clear, concise writing style makes the most complex knots and involved tactics easy to understand. Whether you're a novice or an expert, you will become a better angler by reading Unkart's book.

IT'S AVAILABLE AT WWW.GETGUP.COM

TACTICS, TACKLE, TRICKS, SPREADS, AND RIGGING FOR THE ADVANCED TUNA ANGLER

TUNA FISHING

A MODERN APPROACH FROM THE COCKPIT UP

BY JON MEADE

[ALBACORE * BIGEYE * BLACKFIN * BLUEFIN * YELLOWFIN]

Tuna nuts will want to know about Tuna Fishing: A Modern Approach from the Cockpit Up, by Jon Meade. Capt. Mead—a noted tuna fishing authority who writes for publications including In The Bite, Sport Fishing, and Boating Magazine—grew up in the big game sportfishing community and has worked boats from Ocean City to Palm Beach and beyond. His knowledge and expertise pours out on the pages of this book, which details cutting-edge tricks and techniques professional anglers use to win big-money tournaments and put meat in the box day in and day out. Want proof? No problem—Meade was running the cockpit of the Sea Wolf when the boat took the 181 pound yellowfin that took first place for tuna, and won a cool quarter-mil in the 2006 Mid Atlantic $500,000. He also was running the cockpit when this boat took an 875 pound bluefin tuna and a 210 pound big eye.

AND YES, IT'S AVAILABLE AT WWW.GETGUP.COM

FLOUNDER
Fishing Tactics and Techniques

Keith Kaufman

Former Managing Editor of The Fisherman Magazine and Field
Editor for Chesapeake Angler and The Fisherman Magazines

If you want to know how the pros go after flatfish, then this book is for you. Tackle, tactics, and techniques of the doormat masters are just a few of the secrets exposed in Flounder Fishing Tactics and Techniques. The author Keith Kaufman was the managing editor of The Fisherman magazine for over a decade, and is currently a field editor for both the Chesapeake Angler and The Fisherman magazines. As a professional in the sportfishing industry Keith is respected, and on the water he is feared—by the fish, that is. And one of his favorite species to chase is the tasty, hard-fighting flounder. In his new book he shares all the insight and hard-won knowledge he's accumulated over the years. You want to be a more successful flounder fisherman? This book shows you the way.

IT'S AVAILABLE AT WWW.GETGUP.COM
SPRING 2007

Geared Up is dedicated to bringing saltwater anglers the how-to/where-to information that to date has been impossible to get without putting in years and years of fishing and networking among professional anglers. The books published by Geared Up are full of the tricks, tips and tactics that professional captains and serious anglers usually keep to themselves. Our goal is bringing you the real-world, no BS saltwater fishing information you just can't get anywhere else. If you want to read entertaining fishing stories, get Hemmingway. If you want hard-core how-to/where-to fishing information, get Geared Up. You can find Geared Up's books at our web site (www.getgup.com or www.geareduppublications.com) and in fine tackle shops and book stores. And, we offer the following guarantee: If these books don't help you catch more fish, we'll eat our bait!

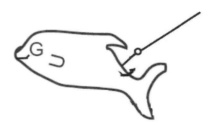